Poems for Gardeners

Poems for Gardeners

Edited by

GERMAINE GREER

Virago

A *Virago* Book

First published in Great Britain by Virago Press

Preface, selection and modernised texts of poems
not in copyright. © Germaine Greer 2003

The moral right of the author has been asserted

A CIP catalogue record for this book is available
from the British Library

ISBN 1 84408 009 9

Typeset in Goudy by M Rules
Printed and bound in Great Britain by
Clays Ltd, St Ives plc

Virago Press
An imprint of
Time Warner Books UK
Brettenham House
Lancaster Place
London WC2E 7EN

www.virago.co.uk

List of Poems

The Garden

The Gardener

The Seasons

The Gardener's Work

The Gardener's Companions

The Gardener's Machinations

The Gardener's Reward

Preface

According to the Scriptures it was God himself who designed and brought into existence the first garden, as the ideal environment for the crown of his creation. He walked in it with Adam before the coming of that garden-buster, Eve, so some, for example, Thomas Edward Brown, famous only for his bad little poem 'My Garden' ('A garden is a lovesome thing, God wot!' etc.) which I have not included, imagine that in a man-made garden one is closer to God, when Scripture itself tells him otherwise.

After his ejection from the Garden of Eden, Adam delved and Eve span, which must mean that there were fleeces to spin, so presumably Adam at some stage managed to corral a few sheep. Herding is holy, and is written into the entire Judaeo-Christian tradition. Abel was a shepherd, King David too, and Christ figured Himself forth in parables as the Good Shepherd. Gardening is the province of Cain, described in the Authorised Version as a 'tiller of the ground'. We may imagine him as the first ever swidden horticulturalist, who slashed and burned and hoed before he could bring his 'fruit of the ground' as an offering to God, who 'had not respect' for it. No reason is given; it is nowhere said that Cain skimped on his offering or offered second-best. Nor is it implied that he worked any harder or less than Abel. Perhaps by gardening Cain tried to emulate God, and that was his offence. Gardeners, whether they are the Dugum Dani struggling to prove their manhood by growing the biggest yams or Alice Oswald's melon grower or David Constantine's miner cossetting his leeks or Ben Jonson's Thomas Palmer, are committed to improving on God's creation.

However it was, Cain was so infuriated by God's favouring Abel that he beat his brother to death. The human race is descended from a murdering gardener, as Douglas Dunn, whose poem 'Gardeners' celebrates others of the ilk, is well aware. Robert Frost reminds us, when he steps on the hoe and it turns into a weapon, that it was Cain's son Tubal-cain who first beat a sword into a ploughshare. That not-quite contradiction is subtly reworked by Seamus Heaney in 'The Pitchfork'.

No gardener is unaware that a garden is first of all a killing-ground. Gardeners distinguish between desirable and undesirable vegetation, and ruthlessly destroy the undesirable which is always the more vigorous. Plants native to the place and admirably adapted to flourish in it without cultivation are dubbed weeds and dug up or poisoned; select plants are favoured over invasive plants, the one indulged and encouraged, the other thinned and lopped. In 'The Morals of Pruning' Ruth Pitter worries about the wounds she inflicts on her grapevine, and in 'The Tall Fruit-Trees' she exults that all her ladders are too short to allow her to cut the old trees down to size. Anna Laetitia Barbauld has to confess that she has slaughtered 'tribes and embryo nations', before finding herself incapable of squashing a single caterpillar after he has walked on her with his 'hairy feet'. James Fenton's experience as a war reporter lies behind his account of the apple-grower poisoning his land with arsenate of lead.

For George Herbert and Rowland Watkyns God is the gardener and we sinners are the plants He lops and prunes. In 'Pot-bound'

Ruth Pitter sees her soul struggling within her body as a plant in need of potting-on, and beseeches the Gardener '(if Gardener there be)' to come to her aid. Theodore Roethke prefers to be gardener rather than plant but he argues on a hint from Gerard Manley Hopkins that the weeds that he struggles to control 'keep the spirit undefiled'. U. A. Fanthope's 'Men on Allotments' are godly beings whose Sunday labours glorify God more effectively than church attendance would do. Anne Ridler is a deeply religious poet who sees her seasons in terms of the liturgical year, as does e. e. cummings who thanks God for giving him spring and redemption on the same day, namely, Easter, though he does not name it.

Most of us whether Christian or otherwise see something virtuous in hard work, and gardening offers plenty of that. Arnold's 'Quiet Work' though not ostensibly about gardening confronts some of the contradictions in gardeners' attitudes to what they do, the endless preparation for things that may never happen, their confidence in the future, and the larger scheme of which the gardener is an unwitting part. Ruth Pitter's die-hards take Arnold's pious scepticism a step further, and find in their flowers and fruits themselves all the justification needed for all their hard work. Duncan Bush comes closest perhaps to what drives gardeners when he celebrates the work in itself, having nothing to show for it but blistered palms. William Empson might appear to make the opposite case, because 'Rolling the Lawn' is hard, repetitive and futile, but it will ultimately be his salvation. Empson would certainly have known and appreciated D. H. Lawrence's celebration of unmown, seeding grass, with its sneer at Walt Whitman.

Two poems by Andrew Marvell, one celebrating the garden as

an ideal state conducive to the 'highest imaginings' and another condemning it as a vicious environment in which genetic modifiers have their ungodly will, spell out the ambivalent morality of gardening. Marvell's mower describes how gardeners first create an artificial space, then artificial conditions within the space, and then use diabolical artifice to create shapes and colours unseen in nature. Yet both Marvell's gardens are the same place: in the first grapes, nectarines, peaches and melons ripen, as in England they will only do against warm walls or under glass. Marvell's imagination revels in contradiction; he is well aware that the gardens in both poems are versions of the paradisaical 'hortus conclusus' and that both in celebrating the one as a solitary retreat and condemning the other he is subverting the Biblical tradition of the garden as an environment ordained by God.

With the never-ending sprawl of suburbia more and more gardens tend to be enclosed, and planted out with gaudy hybrids and exotics more hideous than anything Marvell could have imagined. Norman Nicholson's inner-city garden with its daffodils and ferns eking a living in 'soot and tea-leaves' is something we all can recognise, as too the 'five square feet of bitterness' in which Freda Downie's grandmother grows her grapes and tiger-lilies.

There is another kind of garden, an open-ended garden, which nature flows in and through and control is exercised only intermittently. Such are Clare's cottage garden, where children have transplanted the ox-eye daisies, snowdrops and violets they have found in the wild, and the garden of De La Mare's widow who cultivates weeds. Carol Rumens too forgives her weeds and P. J. Kavanagh pays homage to elder. John Scott of Amwell rejects the exotic gardening of his fashionable Hertfordshire neighbours, for the kind of landscape then being designed by Capability Brown, in which the far prospect and the contiguous agricultural land were both incorporated. In his comic poem 'Amphion' Tennyson mocks himself and the contrivers of specimen and system gardens, in particular the botanical misses next door.

No garden can be really enclosed because wild things will visit it, tunnelling into it like Plath's blue moles, ambling across it like Larkin's hedgehog. Complete control is no more than a fantasy. The gardener has only to die or go away and his turf will succumb to poor drainage and his trimmed bushes become lank leggy trees, as in Hardy's 'Where They Lived'. The realities of death and decay are permanently before the gardener's eyes, and a poem by the late Elizabeth Jennings and another by Phoebe Hesketh both place the gardener's inevitable death as part of the pattern.

For the pagans of classical antiquity gardens were under the aegis of the fertility god Priapus, represented as a herm, a column surmounted by a bearded male bust, and sporting a massive erect penis, as described by Horace. Ruth Pitter is more circumspect, but her 'Aged Cupid' is one and the same. Marvell sees his garden as a sexy place, where a solitary man might be ensnared by amorous vegetation. Solitariness emerges as a condition much prized by gardeners, as poem after poem celebrates the garden as a retreat, from R. S. Thomas's 'place to be lonely for a while', to Nicholas Breton's 'garden ground of grief'. John Burnside's 'Solitary in Autumn' is one of a group of male gardeners who find in their greenhouses and on their allotments an absorption as single-minded as other men might find in train-spotting or Arsenal.

Nathaniel Hookes follows a contrasting tradition in which the garden represents the pleasance, a place for dallying. His garden makes love not to him but to his lady, conspiring to trip her, so that he may give her 'a green gown', by making love to her on the grass. So Coleridge can relax in the 'warm wooings' of a sunny day and even Tennyson can murmur in a dream of exotic sexual inversion in which his beloved will fold herself up and slip into his bosom like a water-lily submerging in an ornamental lake. Hart Crane too knows that 'late amber afternoon' is no time to be alone in a garden. In Jenny Joseph's 'unlooked-for season', a sunny day in the garden in winter is the correlative of sexual passion in the third age. Similarly we find David Constantine describing summer pushing 'her tongue into the winter's throat'. Robert Frost describes himself as 'slave to a springtime passion for the earth', and does not shrink from the sexual connotations of sowing seed in the garden, but here it is the seedling itself which is the object of his desire. Theodore Roethke too feels an excitement about the slow phenomena of plant propagation that is, if very subtly, distinctly Priapic. Fleur Adcock's description of slugs mating, though it represents a gardener's nightmare, projects something like envy of creatures whose bodies are 'each a complete erogenous zone'. Something similar informs Thom Gunn's tribute to the passion of a snail and Vicki Feaver's interpreting the winking of a glow-worm's abdomen as Molly Bloom's famous 'yes yes yes'.

My intention in compiling this collection has been to assemble a group of poems that would mean more to gardeners than they would to people who don't garden. I have tended to concentrate on poems in which gardens stand for themselves and are not analogues or allegories of something else; even the obviously moralising poems have had to show some awareness of and concern for what goes on in gardens before I would accept them for inclusion. Critics writing about gardening poems, who are not themselves gardeners, may have interpreted some or all of these poems as encoded autobiography or aesthetics or politics, and may have been justified in doing so. I have been looking for something more, a truth to the sensuous experience and the emotion of gardening itself, something in each poem that other gardeners, who are more numerous than professors of literature, might recognise, and smile – or wince.

Germaine Greer
2003

The Garden

R. S. THOMAS

The Garden

It is a gesture against the wild,
The ungovernable sea of grass;
A place to remember love in,
To be lonely for a while;
To forget the voices of children
Calling from a locked room;
To substitute for the care
Of one querulous human
Hundreds of dumb needs.

It is the old kingdom of man.
Answering to their names,
Out of the soil the buds come,
The silent detonations
Of power wielded without sin.

NICHOLAS GRIMALD

The Garden

The issue of great Jove, draw near you Muses nine;
Help us to praise the blissful plot of garden ground so fine.
The garden gives good food and aid for leeches' cure;
The garden, full of great delight, its master doth allure.
Sweet salad herbs be here, and herbs of every kind;
The ruddy grapes, the seemly fruits, be here at hand to find.
Here pleasance wanteth not to make a man full fain;
Here marvellous the mixture is, of solace and of gain.
To water sundry seeds, the furrow by the way
A running river trilling down with liquor can convey.
Behold, with lively hue, fair flowers that shine so bright;
With riches, like the orient gems, they paint the mould in sight.
Bees humming with soft sound (their murmur is so small)
Of blooms and blossoms suck the tops, on dewèd leaves they fall.
The creeping vine holds down her own bewedded elms
And, wandering out with branches thick, reeds folded
    overwhelms.
Trees spread their coverts wide, with shadows fresh and gay;
Full well their branchèd boughs defend the fervent sun away.
Birds chatter, and some chirp, and some sweet tunes do yield;
All mirthful with their songs so blithe they make both air and
    field.
The garden it allures, it feeds and glads the sprite;

From heavy hearts all doleful dumps the garden chaseth quite.
Strength it restores to limbs, draws and fulfils the sight,
With cheer revives the senses all, and maketh labour light.
Oh, what delights to us the garden ground doth bring,
Seed, leaf, flower, fruit, herb, bee and tree, and more than I may
    sing.

(MODERNISED VERSION © G. GREER)

NICHOLAS BRETON

A Strange Description of a rare Garden Plot

My garden ground of grief where self-will's seeds are sown,
Whereof come up the weeds of woe, that joys have overgrown,
With patience paled around, to keep in secret spite,
And quick-set round about with care, to keep out all delight.

Four quarters squarèd out I find in sundry sort
Whereof according to their kinds I mean to make report:
The first, the knot of love drawn even by true desire,
Like as it were two hearts in one, and yet both would be nigher.

The herb is callèd hyssop, the juice of such a taste
As with the sour makes sweet conceits to fly away too fast.
The borders round about are set with privet sweet
Where never bird but nightingale presumed to set her feet.

From this I stepped aside unto the knot of care
Which so was crossed with strange conceits as tongue cannot
declare.
The herb was called thyme, which set out all that knot,
And like a maze methought it was when in its crooks I got.

The borders round about are savory unsweet,
An herb not much, in my conceit, for such a knot unmeet.
From this to friendship's knot I stepped and took the view
How it was drawn, and then again in order how it grew.

The course was not unlike a kind of hand-in-hand
But many fingers were away that there should seem to stand.
The herb that set the knot was pennyroyal round,
And as me seemed it grew full close and near unto the ground.

And parchèd here and there so that it seemèd not
Full as it should have been indeed, a perfect friendship knot;
Hereat I paused a while, and took a little view
Of an odd quarter drawn in beds where herbs and flowers grew.

The flowers were buttons fine for bachelors to wear,
And by those flowers there grew an herb was called maiden-hair.

Amid this garden ground, a conduit strange I found
Which water fetched from sorrow's spring to water all the
ground.
To this my heavy house, the dungeon of distress,
Where fainting heart lies panting still despairing of redress,

Whence from my window, lo, this sad prospect I have,
A piece of ground whereon to gaze would bring one to his grave.
Lo, thus the welcome spring that others lends delight
Doth make me die, to think I lie, thus drownèd in despite,

That up I cannot rise and come abroad to thee,
My fellow sweet, with whom God knows how oft I wish to be,
And thus, in haste, adieu. My heart is grown so sore
And care so crooks my fingers' ends that I can write no more.

(MODERNISED VERSION © G. GREER)

ANDREW MARVELL

The Garden

How vainly men themselves amaze
To win the palm, the oak or bays,
And their incessant labours see
Crowned with some single herb or tree,
Whose short and narrow vergèd shade
Does prudently their toil upbraid,
While all flowers and all trees do close
To weave the garlands of repose.

Fair Quiet, I have found thee here,
And Innocence, thy sister dear.
Mistaken long I sought you then
In busy companies of men.
Your sacred plants, if here below,
Only among the plants will grow.
Society is all but rude
To this delicious solitude.

No white nor red was ever seen
So amorous as this lovely green.
Fond lovers, cruel as their flame,
Cut in these trees their mistress' name.
Little, alas! they know or heed
How far these beauties hers exceed.

Fair trees, whene'er your barks I wound
Shall no name but your own be found.

When we have run our passions' heat,
Love hither makes his best retreat.
The gods that mortal beauty chase,
Still in a tree did end their race.
Apollo hunted Daphne so
Only that she might laurel grow,
And Pan did after Syrinx speed
Not as a nymph but for a reed.

What wondrous life in this I lead!
Ripe apples drop about my head;
The luscious clusters of the vine
Upon my mouth do crush their wine;
The nectarine and curious peach
Into my hands themselves do reach;
Stumbling on melons as I pass,
Ensnared with flowers, I fall on grass.

Meanwhile the mind, from pleasure less,
Withdraws into its happiness,
The mind, that ocean where each kind
Does straight its own resemblance find,
Yet it creates, transcending these,
Far other worlds and other seas,
Annihilating all that's made
To a green thought in a green shade.

Here at the fountain's sliding foot
Or at some fruit-tree's mossy root,
Casting the body's vest aside,
My soul into the boughs does glide.
There, like a bird, it sits and sings,
Then whets and combs its silver wings,
And, till prepared for longer flight,
Waves in its plumes the various light.

Such was that happy garden state
When man there lived without a mate.
After a place so pure and sweet,
What other help could yet be meet?
But 'twas beyond a mortal's share
To wander solitary there.
Two Paradises 'twere in one
To live in Paradise alone.

(MODERNISED VERSION © G. GREER)

JOHN CLARE

The Cottage Garden

The shrill bat there its evening circles makes
And scouts round trees and shed for many an hour.
The yellow goslings dabble in the lakes,
The puddley produce of a hasty shower.
There the black house bee sucks the garden flower
Till after sunset, for its home is nigh,
And white moth sheltered in its eldern bower,
Woken ere the sun drops from the western sky,
Dances in the leaves from daylight's closing eye.

Before each door, on each grass screeded spot,
Mottled with wormwood tufts and mallow blooms,
The little child (dread winter's frowns forgot)
To the soft sunshine of the summer comes.
Sweet is the sky to shelter's smoky rooms,
And glad he laughs, at freedom's will to play,
And many a bee its little malice hums
Amid the blossoms which he bears away,
Uncloying spoils of childhood's holiday.

Go there in summer. Though stiff painted pride
Disdains the picture, thou wilt find it fair,
And sweet as e'er thy curious eye descried
'Twould find the beauties summer painteth there.

To its loved walls, bees do their honey bear
And hum a tune of summer poesy.
The sparrow chirps its household music there,
And children's merry shouts have nought but joys to share.

Spring seems in raptures with the lovely spot,
And hastes her footsteps to its peace again,
And wildflowers children plant around the cot
Show earlier flowers than those upon the plain.
The gold-eyed daisy with its ruddy stain
Will even venture ere the frosts are by,
And on the snow-drop's tiny couch remain
And, neath a privet hedge soft sheltering nigh,
The violet often blooms, nor waits an april sky.

Around its walls the woodbine idly weaves,
Or greener shades of the untamed vine
That wildly mounts the houseleek-covered eaves,
And round the chimney if unchecked would twine,
And in the garden night-brown columbine
And pink and rose thy charmèd sight shall hail,
And mottled marjoram tufts that smell divine,
These deck the cot. And, leisure to regale,
Toil nears its sodded bench, and tells its evening tale.

(EDITED VERSION © G. GREER)

THOMAS HARDY

Where They Lived

Dishevelled leaves creep down
   Upon that bank to-day,
Some green, some yellow, and some pale brown;
   The wet bents bob and sway;
The once warm slippery turf is sodden
   Where we laughingly sat or lay.

The summerhouse is gone,
   Leaving a weedy space;
The bushes that veiled it once have grown
   Gaunt trees that interlace,
Through whose lank limbs I see too clearly
   The nakedness of the place.

And where were hills of blue,
   Blind drifts of vapour blow,
And the names of former dwellers few,
   If any, people know,
And instead of a voice that called, 'Come in, Dears,'
   Time calls, 'Pass below!'

GEORGE HERBERT

Paradise — The Gardener's Prayer

I bless thee, Lord, because I grow
Among thy trees, which in a row
To Thee both fruit and order owe.

What open force or hidden charm
Can blast my fruit or bring me harm
While the enclosure is Thine arm?

Enclose me still for fear I start.
Be to me rather sharp and tart
Than let me want Thy hand and art.

When Thou dost greater judgments spare,
And with Thy knife but prune and pare,
Even fruitful trees more fruitful are.

Such sharpness shows the sweetest friend;
Such cuttings rather heal than rend,
And such beginnings touch their end.

(MODERNISED VERSION © G. GREER)

JOHN SCOTT OF AMWELL

The Garden – Epistle to a Friend

From Whitby's rocks steep rising o'er the main,
From Eska's vales, or Ewecot's lonely plain,
Say, rove thy thoughts to Amwell's distant bowers.
To mark how pass thy friend's sequestered hours?

   'Perhaps,' thinkst thou, 'He seeks his pleasing scenes
Of winding walks, smooth lawns and shady greens,
Where China's willow hangs its foliage fair,
And Po's tall poplar waves its top in air,
And the dark maple spreads its umbrage wide,
And the white bench adorns the basin side.
At morn perhaps he sits to view
The bank's neat slope, the water's silver hue,
Where midst thick oaks the subterraneous way
To the arched grot admits a feeble ray,
Where glossy pebbles pave the varied floors,
And rough flint walls are decked with shells and ores,
And silvery pearls spread o'er the roofs so high
Glimmer like faint stars in a twilight sky.
From noon's fierce glare, perhaps, he pleased retires,
Indulging musings that the place inspires.
Now where the airy octagon ascends
And wide the prospect o'er the vale extends,
'Midst evening's calm intent perhaps he stands

And looks o'er all that length of sun-gilt lands,
Of bright green pastures stretched by rivers clear
And willow groves or osier islands near.'

Alas, my friend, how strangely men mistake
Who guess what others most their pleasure make!
These garden scenes which Fashion o'er our plains
Spreads round the villas of our wealthy swains,
Though Envy grudge or Friendship wish to share,
They claim but little of their owners' care.
For me, my groves not oft my steps invite
And far less oft they fail to offend my sight.
In vain the senna waves its glossy gold;
In vain the cistus' spotted flowers unfold;
In vain the acacia's snowy bloom depends;
In vain the sumach's scarlet spike ascends;
In vain the woodbine's spicy tufts disclose,
And green slopes redden with the blushing rose.
These neat-shorn hawthorns' useless verdant bound,
This long straight walk, that pool's unmeaning round,
These short curved paths that twist beneath the trees
Disgust the eye and make the whole displease.

'No scene like this,' I say, 'did Nature raise,
Brown's fancy form, or Walpole's judgment praise.
No prototype for this did I survey
In Woollett's landscapes or in Mason's lay.'

But might thy genius, friend, an Eden frame,

Profuse of beauty and secure from blame,
Where round the lawn might wind the varied way,
Now lost in gloom, and now with prospect gay,
Now screened with clumps of green for winter bowers,
Now edged with sunny banks for summer flowers,
Now led by crystal lakes with lilies dressed
Or where light temples court the step to rest,
Time's gradual change or tempest's sudden rage
There with thy peace perpetual war would wage.
That tyrant oak, whose arms so far o'ergrow,
Shades some poor shrub that pines with drought below;
These rampant elms, those hazels branching wide,
Crowd the broad pine, the spiry larix hide.

That lilac brow, where May's unsparing hand
Bade one vast swell of purple bloom expand,
Soon past its prime, shows signs of quick decay,
The naked stem and scantly covered spray.
Fierce Boreas calls, and Ruin waits his call;
Thy fair catalpa's broken branches fall,
Thy soft magnolia mourns her blasted green
And blighted laurel's yellowing leaves are seen.

But Discontent alone, thou'lt say, complains
For ill success, where none perfection gains.
True is the charge, but from that tyrant's sway
What art, what power can e'er redeem our day?
To me, indeed, short ease he sometimes yields,
When my lone walk surrounds the rural fields.

There no past errors of my own upbraid,
No time, no wealth expended unrepaid.
There Nature dwells, and throws profuse around
Each pastoral sight and every pastoral sound,
From Spring's green copse that pours the cuckoo's strain
And evening bleatings of the fleecy train,
To Autumn's yellow field and clamorous horn
That wakes the slumbering harvesters at dawn.
There Fancy too with fond delighted eyes
Sees o'er the scene ideal people rise.
There calm Contentment in his cot reclined
Hears the grey poplars whisper in the wind.
There Love's sweet songs adown the echoing dale
To Beauty's ear conveys the tender tale,
And there Devotion lifts his brow to Heaven
With grateful thanks for many a blessing given.

Thus oft through Maylan's shady lane I stray,
Trace Rushgreen's paths or Postwood's winding way.
Thus oft to Eastfield's airy height I haste
(All well-known spots thy feet have frequent traced!)
While Memory, as my sight around I cast,
Suggests the pleasing thought of moments past,
Or Hope amid the future forms again
The dream of bliss Experience broke in vain.

(MODERNISED VERSION © G. GREER)

NORMAN NICHOLSON

A Garden Enclosed

Hortus Conclusus

Red as old plant pots, tall
As the reach of the scrag-arm creeper,
The bricks of the wall
(Greened and grained with moss)
Bar the yard from the street.
Blue slate flags
Lay cracks of black that cross
In a pattern and puzzle for feet,
And rag-tag tiles,
Up-ended in a row,
Hold soil where daffodils
And *Osmunda regalis* grow.

Outside, clouds
Explode and condense again;
The Baptist Chapel steeple shakes
Under a gravel of rain;
The sea regurgitates its dead,
And the horizon breaks
With earth-spouts and water-quakes.

But here where soot and tea-leaves
Fertilise the ferns,

And the pale-green butterfly
Arranges her chess-set of eggs;
Where starlings boil on the eaves,
And tits with rubber-coated legs
Wire themselves to the clothes-pegs —
Here let the Holy Child
Eena-meena-mumble words
That make the wild
Wind creep like a sheep-dog.
And let His lifted fingers
Magnetise the feet of birds,
And His bright knees run
Round leaf and latch and dust-bin
Till zinc, rust and window-box shine
    eye to eye with the sun.

NATHANIEL HOOKES

To Amanda Walking in the Garden

And now what monarch would not gardener be,
My fair Amanda's stately gait to see?
How her feet tempt! How soft and light she treads,
Fearing to wake the flowers from their beds!
Yet from their sweet green pillows everywhere,
They start and gaze about to see my fair.
Look at yon flower yonder, how it grows,
Sensibly! How it opes its leaves and blows,
Puts its best Easter clothes on, neat and gay—
Amanda's presence makes it holiday!
Look how on tiptoe that fair lily stands
To look on thee, and court thy whiter hands
To gather it! I saw in yonder crowd—
That tulip bed of which Dame Flora's proud—
A short dwarf flower did enlarge its stalk,
And shoot an inch to see Amanda walk.
Nay, look, my fairest! Look how fast they grow
Into a scaffold-method spring! As though,
Riding to Parliament, were to be seen
In pomp and state some royal amorous queen.
The gravelled walks, though even as a die,
Lest some loose pebble should offensive lie,
Quilt themselves o'er with downy moss for thee;
The walls are hanged with blossomed tapestry

To hide their nakedness when looked upon;
The maiden fig-tree puts Eve's apron on;
The broad-leaved sycamore, and every tree,
Shakes like the trembling asp, and bends to thee,
And each leaf proudly strives, with fresher air
To fan the curlèd tresses of thy hair.
Nay, and the bee, too, with his wealthy thigh,
Mistakes his hive, and to thy lips doth fly,
Willing to treasure up his honey there,
Where honeycombs so sweet and plenty are.
Look how that pretty modest columbine
Hangs down its head, to view those feet of thine!
See the fond motion of the strawberry
Creeping on th' earth, to go along with thee!
The lovely violet makes after too,
Unwilling yet, my dear, to part with you;
The knot-grass and the daisies catch thy toes,
To kiss my fair one's feet before she goes;
All court and wish me lay Amanda down,
And give my dear a new green-flowered gown.
    Come, let me kiss thee falling, kiss at rise,
    Thou in the garden, I in Paradise.

ALFRED, LORD TENNYSON

Amphion

My father left a park to me,
    But it is wild and barren,
A garden too with scarce a tree,
    And waster than a warren.
Yet say the neighbours when they call,
    It is not bad but good land,
And in it is the germ of all
    That grows within the woodland.

O had I lived when song was great
    In days of old, Amphion,
And ta'en my fiddle to the gate,
    Nor cared for seed or scion!
And had I lived when song was great,
    And legs of trees were limber,
And ta'en my fiddle to the gate,
    And fiddled in the timber!

'Tis said he had a tuneful tongue,
    Such happy intonation,
Wherever he sat down and sung
    He left a small plantation.
Wherever in a lonely grove
    He set up his forlorn pipes,
The gouty oak began to move,
    And flounder into hornpipes.

The mountain stirr'd its bushy crown
    And, as tradition teaches,
Young ashes pirouetted down
    Coquetting with young beeches
And briony-vine and ivy-wreath
    Ran forward to his rhyming,
And from the valleys underneath
    Came little copses climbing.

The linden broke her ranks and rent
    The woodbine wreaths that bind her,
And down the middle, buzz! she went
    With all her bees behind her.
The poplars, in long order due,
    With cypress promenaded,
The shock-head willows two and two
    By rivers gallopaded.

Came wet-shod alder from the wave,
    Came yews, a dismal coterie;
Each pluck'd his one foot from the grave,
    Poussetting with a sloe-tree.
Old elms came breaking from the vine.
    The vine stream'd out to follow,
And, sweating rosin plump'd the pine
    From many a cloudy hollow.

And wasn't it a sight to see,
    When, ere his song was ended,
Like some great landslip, tree by tree,
    The country-side descended

And shepherds from the mountain-eaves
   Look'd down, half-pleased, half-frighten'd,
As dash'd about the drunken leaves
   The random sunshine lighten'd!

Oh, nature first was fresh to men,
   And wanton without measure,
So youthful and so flexile then,
   You moved her at your pleasure.
Twang out, my fiddle! shake the twigs!
   And make her dance attendance;
Blow, flute, and stir the stiff-set sprigs,
   And scirrhous roots and tendons.

'Tis vain! in such a brassy age
   I could not move a thistle;
The very sparrows in the hedge
   Scarce answer to my whistle,
Or at the most, when three-parts-sick
   With strumming and with scraping,
A jackass heehaws from the rick,
   The passive oxen gaping.

But what is that I hear? a sound
   Like sleepy counsel pleading;
O Lord!—'tis in my neighbour's ground,
   The modern Muses reading.
They read Botanic Treatises,
   And Works on Gardening thro' there,
And Methods of transplanting trees
   To look as if they grew there.

The wither'd Misses! how they prose
    O'er books of travell'd seamen,
And show you slips of all that grows
    From England to Van Diemen.
They read in arbours clipt and cut,
    And alleys, faded places,
By squares of tropic summer shut
    And warm'd in crystal cases.

But these, tho' fed with careful dirt,
    Are neither green nor sappy;
Half-conscious of the garden-squirt,
    The spindlings look unhappy.
Better to me the meanest weed
    That blows upon its mountain,
The vilest herb that runs to seed
    Beside its native fountain.

And I must work thro' months of toil,
    And years of cultivation,
Upon my proper patch of soil
    To grow my own plantation.
I'll take the showers as they fall,
    I will not vex my bosom:
Enough if at the end of all
    A little garden blossom.

ANNA WICKHAM

A House in Hampstead

My house is damp as damp can be,
It stands on London clay.
And if I move unthinkingly
It shakes in a most alarming way,
Mayhap it will all come down on me
One day.
But through the window I can see
The most enchanting apple-tree.
In spring-time, there are daffodils
And primroses on little hills,
And high within my apple-tree
A blackbird comes and sings to me;
On the black branch he sits and sings
Of birds and nests and eggs and things.
I can't remember as I hear
That old grey London lies so near.

The Gardener

HORACE

Book I, Satire VIII – Complaint of Priapus

'Olim truncus eram ficulnus, inutile lignum.'

IN days of yore our godship stood,
A very worthless log of wood,
The joiner doubting, or to shape us
Into a stool, or a Priapus,
At length resolved, for reasons wise,
Into a god to bid me rise;
And now to birds and thieves I stand
A terror great. With ponderous hand,
And something else as red as scarlet,
I fright away each filching varlet.
The birds, that view with awful dread
The reeds, fast stuck into my head,
Far from the garden take their flight,
Nor on the trees presume to light.

    In coffins vile the herd of slaves
Were hither brought to crowd their graves;
And once in this detested ground
A common tomb the vulgar found;
Buffoons and spendthrifts, vile and base,
Together rotted here in peace.
A thousand feet the front extends,
Three hundred deep in rear it bends,
And yonder column plainly shows

No more unto its heirs it goes.
But now we breathe a purer air,
And walk the sunny terrace fair,
Where once the ground with bones was white,
—With human bones, a ghastly sight!
  But, oh! nor thief, nor savage beast,
That used these gardens to infest,
E'er gave me half such cares and pains
As they, who turn poor people's brains
With venomed drugs and magic lay—
These I can never fright away;
For when the beauteous queen of night
Uplifts her head adorned with light
Hither they come, pernicious crones!
To gather poisonous herbs and bones.
  Canidia with dishevelled hair
(Black was her robe, her feet were bare),
With Sagana, infernal dame!
Her elder sister, hither came.
With yellings dire they filled the place,
And hideous pale was either's face.
Soon with their nails they scraped the ground,
And filled a magic trench profound
With a black lamb's thick-streaming gore,
Whose members with their teeth they tore,
That they may charm the sprites to tell
Some curious anecdotes from hell.
The beldams then two figures brought;
Of wool and wax the forms were wrought

The woollen was erect and tall,
And scourged the waxen image small,
Which dying air just gasping stood.

On Hecate one beldam calls;
The other to the Furies bawls,
While serpents crawl along the ground,
And Stygian she-dogs howl around.
The blushing moon, to shun the sight,
Behind a tomb withdrew her light.

Oh! if I lie, may ravens shed
Their ordure on my sacred head!

Not to be tedious, or repeat
How flats and sharps in concert meet,
With which the ghosts and hags maintain
A dialogue of passing strain;
Or how, to hide the tooth of snake
And beard of wolf, the ground they break:
Or how the fire of magic seized
The waxen form, and how it blazed;
Mark how my vengeance I pursued
For all I heard, for all I viewed.

Loud as a bladder bursts its wind,
Dreadful it thundered from behind.
To town they scampered, struck with fear,
This lost her teeth, and that her hair.
They dropped the bracelets from their arms,
Their incantations, herbs and charms;
Whoe'er had seen them in their flight
Had burst with laughing at the sight.

RUTH PITTER

Aged Cupid

The old man with the washed cord breeks,
The man who cuts the hedge so clean,
The little man with rosy cheeks,
The man whose merry eyes have been
Never more bright, if far more keen;
The man who keeps the bonfire in,
Keeps the great heap through days and weeks
Smouldering in secret, slow and sure;
Who chops a sapling with his bill
Down in a trice—the sly demure
Old laughing man who sits so still,
Subtly achieving all his will,
Who having tools cannot be poor:

Who turns the least mishap to mirth,
Shrieking at withered cucumbers,
And doubled up because of dearth
In what his grim old girl calls hers—
The lagging parsley-bed, or fine
Sweet-peas gone droughty, bristling sere
Where last week saw a brilliant line;
Or seedling beets one morning here,
The next day eaten by the flea—
Convulsive spleen to you and me,

But one more heaven-sent joke to he:

The women's favourite, pretty lad,
And pretty still at seventy-four,
He'd like to go upon the gad,
To make the lasses laughing-mad,
As he has often done before;
To make them dance to violin
Or the heart-wiling concertina
Till legs grow weak and breath comes thin
And even the fattest wench is leaner:
Till the mad settle dances too,
And dust befogs the whirling mazes,
And the choked lamp-wick splutters blue,
And beer and money go like blazes—

What is he up to now? Go see;
Creep on the grass without a sound.
So rapt and so intent is he
He's brewing some young devilry—
Good Lord! Look what the man has found!
A well-grown Viper, which he nips
Behind the head, with a fork
Of the bat-willow's limber tips
Pins to the earth—what devil's work!
It is for his staid son to find.
At evening when he weeding goes,
Under the dewy favourite Rose
The furious serpent will be twined:

He'll howl with horror first, then see
The artifice, and bawl with rage,
While the old rogue, I will engage,
Will almost weep for ecstasy:
Come, girls, and tell me, who is he?

ROWLAND WATKYNS

The Gardener

Mary prevents the day. She rose to weep
And see the bed where Jesus lay asleep.
She found out Whom she sought, but doth not know
Her Master's face. He is the Gardener now.
This Gardener Eden's garden did compose
For which the chiefest flowers and plants He chose.
He took great care to have sweet rivers run
To enrich the ground where He His work begun.
He is the gardener still, and knoweth how
To make the lilies and the roses grow.
He knows the time to set, and when to remove
His living plants to make them better prove.
He hath His pruning-knife, when we grow wild,
To tame our nature and make us more mild.
He curbs His dearest children. When 'tis need,
He cuts His choicest vine and makes it bleed.
He weeds the poisonous herbs which clog the ground.
He knows the rotten hearts, He knows the sound.
The Blessed Virgin was the pleasant bower
This Gardener lodged in His appointed hour.
Before His birth, His garden was the womb;
In death, He in a garden chose His tomb.

(MODERNISED VERSION © G. GREER)

GEORGE WILLIAM FREDERICK HOWARD, VISCOUNT MORPETH

To a Jasmine-Tree in the Court of Nawarth Castle

MY slight and slender jasmine-tree,
 That bloomest on my border tower,
Thou art more dearly loved by me
 Than all the wreaths of fairy bower:
I ask not, while I near thee dwell,
 Arabia's spice, or Syria's rose,
Thy light festoons more freshly smell,
 Thy virgin white more freshly glows.

My mild and winsome jasmine-tree,
 That climbest up the dark grey wall,
Thy tiny flowrets seem in glee,
 Like silver spray-drops, down to fall:
Say, did they from their leaves thus peep,
 When mail'd moss-troopers rode the hill,
When helmed warders paced the keep,
 And bugles blew for Belted Will?

My free and feathery jasmine-tree,
 Within the fragrance of thy breath,
Yon dungeon grated to its key,

And the chain'd captive pined for death.
On border fray, on feudal crime,
   I dream not, while I gaze on thee;
The chieftains of that stern old time
   Could ne'er have loved a jasmine-tree.

DOUGLAS DUNN

Gardeners

England, Loamshire, 1789: *A gardener speaks,*
in the grounds of a great house, to his Lordship.

Gardens, gardens, and we are gardeners . . .
Razored hedgerow, flowers, those planted trees
Whose avenues conduct a greater ease
Of shadow to your own and ladies' skins
And tilt this Nature to magnificence
And natural delight. But pardon us,
My Lord, if we reluctantly admit
Our horticulture not the whole of it,
Forgetting, that for you, this elegance
Is not our work, but your far tidier Sense.

Out of humiliation comes that sweet
Humility that does no good. We know
Our coarser artistries will make things grow.
Others design the craftsmanship we fashion
To please your topographical possession.
A small humiliation – Yes, we eat,
Our crops and passions tucked out of the view
Across a shire, the name of which is you,
Where every native creature runs upon
Hills, moors and meadows which your named eyes own.

Our eyes are nameless, generally turned
Towards the earth our fingers sift all day –
Your day, your earth, your eyes, wearing away
Not earth, eyes, days, but scouring, forcing down
What lives in us and which you cannot own.
One of us heard the earth cry out. It spurned
His hands. It threw stones in his face, We found
That man, my Lord, and he was mad. We bound
His hands together and we heard him say –
'Not me! Not me who cries!' We took away

That man – remember, Lord? – and then we turned,
Hearing your steward order us return,
His oaths, and how you treated us with scorn.
They call this grudge. Let me hear you admit
That in the country that's but half of it.
Townsmen will wonder, when your house was burned,
We did not burn your gardens and undo
What likes of us did for the likes of you;
We did not raze this garden that we made,
Although we hanged you somewhere in its shade.

JOHN BURNSIDE

The Solitary in Autumn

I am standing out in the yard
at the end of October,
building a fire of drifted leaves and twigs,
letters for kindling, apples amongst the flames,
the last of summer, dropping through the embers.

There is that perfume in the shade
that is almost viburnum,
traces of snow and water in the light,
a blankness along the canal
that waits to be filled

and, given the silence, given the promise of frost,
I might have welcomed this as something else:
the taste of windfalls moving on the stream
a faint god's partial emergence
through willow and alder.

The riverbank darkens and fades.
The garden recovers its creatures: slow worms and frogs
and blackbirds sifting the dead
in the still of the damsons.
Across the river, evening bleeds the trees,

my neighbour's garden blurs to smoke and rain;
sometimes I think that someone else is there,
standing in his own yard, raking leaves,
or bending to a clutch of twigs and straw
to breathe a little life into the fire.

FREDA DOWNIE

Her Garden

My grandmother grew tiny grapes and tiger-lilies,
But there is no sentimental cut to her garden
Through a fat album or remembered lane;
Only interior voyages made on London ferries

Paddling the Thames' wicked brew to Silvertown,
Where regular as boot boys, the factories
Blacked her house every day, obscured the skies
And the town's sweet name at the railway station.

Between ships parked at the end of the road
And factory gates, she kept her home against soot,
Kept her garden colours in spite of it –
Five square feet of bitterness in a paved yard

Turned to the silent flowering of her will,
Loaded with dusty beauty and natural odours,
Cinnamon lilies, and the vine roots hanging grapes,
Sour as social justice, on the wash-house wall.

DAVID CONSTANTINE

The Pitman's Garden

(for Bill and Diane Williamson)

Man called Teddy had a garden in
The ruins of Mary Magdalen
By Baxter's Scrap. Grew leeks. What leeks need is
Plenty of shite and sunshine. Sunshine's His
Who gave His only begotten Son to give
Or not but shite is up to us who live
On bread and meat and veg and every day
While Baxter fished along the motorway
For write-offs Teddy arrived with bags of it
From home, which knackered him, the pit
Having blacked his lungs. But Baxter towed in wrecks
On their hind-legs with dolls and busted specs
And things down backs of seats still in and pressed
Them into oxo cubes and Teddy addressed
His ranks of strapping lads and begged them grow
Bonnier and bonnier. Before the show
For fear of slashers he made his bed up there
Above the pubs, coughing on the night air,
Like the Good Shepherd Teddy lay
Under the stars, hearing the motorway,
Hearing perhaps the concentrated lives
Of family cars in Baxter's iron hives.

Heard Baxter's dog howl like a coyote
And sang to his leeks 'Nearer my God to Thee'.
He lays his bearded beauties out. Nothing
On him is so firm and white, but he can bring
These for a common broth and eat his portion.

Leaving town, heading for the M1,
Watch out for the pitman's little garden in
The ruined fold of Mary Magdalen.

U. A. FANTHORPE

Men on Allotments

As mute as monks, tidy as bachelors,
They manicure their little plots of earth.
Pop music from the council house estate
Counterpoints with the Sunday-morning bells,
But neither siren voice has power for these
Drab solitary men who spend their time
Kneeling, or fetching water, soberly,
Or walking softly down a row of beans.

Like drill-sergeants, they measure their recruits.
The infant sprig receives the proper space
The manly fullgrown cauliflower will need.
And all must toe the line here; stem and leaf,
As well as root, obey the rule of string.
Domesticated tilth aligns itself
In sweet conformity; but head in air
Soars the unruly loveliness of beans.

They visit hidden places of the earth
When tenderly with fork and hand they grope
To lift potatoes, and the round, flushed globes
Tumble like pearls out of the moving soil.
They share strange intuitions, know how much
Patience and energy and sense of poise

It takes to be an onion; and they share
The subtle benediction of the beans.

They see the casual holiness that spreads
Along obedient furrows. Cabbages
Unfurl their veined and rounded fans in joy,
And buds of sprouts rejoice along their stalks.
The ferny tops of carrots, stout red stems
Of beetroot, zany sunflowers with blond hair
And bloodshot faces, shine like seraphim
Under the long flat fingers of the beans.

RUTH PITTER

The Diehards

We go, in winter's biting wind,
On many a short-lived winter day,
With aching back but willing mind
To dig and double-dig the clay.

All in November's soaking mist
We stand and prune the naked tree,
While all our love and interest
Seem quenched in blue-nosed misery.

We go in withering July
To ply the hard incessant hoe;
Panting beneath the brazen sky
We sweat and grumble, but we go.

We go to plead with grudging men,
And think it is a bit of luck
When we can wangle now and then
A load or two of farmyard muck.

What do we look for as reward?
Some little sounds, and scents, and scenes:
A small hand darting strawberry-ward,
A woman's apron full of greens.

A busy neighbour, forced to stay
By sight and smell of wallflower-bed;
The plum-trees on an autumn day,
Yellow, and violet, and red.

Tired people sitting on the grass,
Lulled by the bee, drugged by the rose,
While all the little winds that pass
Tell them the honeysuckle blows.

The sense that we have brought to birth
Out of the cold and heavy soil,
These blessed fruits and flowers of earth
Is large reward for all our toil.

ELIZABETH JENNINGS

Her Garden

Not at the full moon will she pick those flowers
For sudden shade indoors would make them wilt.
The petals would drop down on polished wood
Adding another element to decay
Which all her old rooms are infected with.

Only outside she can put off the course
Of her disease. She has the garden built
Within high walls so no one can intrude.
When people pass she only hears the way
Their footsteps sound, ever their closer breath.

But in her borders she observes the powers
Of bud and branch, forgetting how she felt
When, blood within her veins like sap, she stood,
Her arms like branches bare above the day
And all the petals strewn along her path.

No matter now for she has bridged the pause
Between fruition and decay. She'll halt
A little in her garden while a mood
Of peace so fills her that she cannot say
Whether it is the flowers' life or her death.

PHOEBE HESKETH

Death of a Gardener

He rested through the Winter, watched the rain
On his cold garden, slept, awoke to snow
Padding the window, thatching the roof again
With silence. He was grateful for the slow
Nights and undemanding days; the dark
Protected him; the pause grew big with cold.
Mice in the shed scuffled like leaves; a spark
Hissed from his pipe as he dreamed beside the fire.
All at once light sharpened; earth drew breath,
Stirred; and he woke to strangeness that was Spring,
Stood on the grass, felt movement underneath
Like a child in the womb; hope troubled him to bring
Barrow and spade once more to the waiting soil.
Slower his lift and thrust; a blackbird filled
Long intervals with song; a worm could coil
To safety underneath the hesitant blade.
Hands tremulous as cherry branches kept
Faith with struggling seedlings till the earth
Kept faith with him, claimed him as he slept
Cold in the sun beside his upright spade.

BEN JONSON

To Thomas Palmer

When late, grave Palmer, these thy grafts and flowers,
So well disposed by thy auspicious hand,
Were made the objects to my weaker powers,
I could not but in admiration stand.
First, thy success did strike my sense with wonder
That 'mongst so many plants transplanted hither,
Not one but thrives, in spite of storms and thunder,
Unseason'd frosts or the most envious weather.
Then I admired the rare and precious use
Thy skill hath made of rank despisèd weeds,
Whilst other souls convert to base abuse
The sweetest simples and most sovereign seeds.
Next, that which rapt me was, I might behold
How like the carbuncle in Aaron's breast,
The seven-fold flower of art, more rich than gold,
Did sparkle forth in centre of the rest.
Thus, as a ponderous thing in water cast
Extendeth circles into infinites,
Still making that the greatest that is last,
Till the one hath drowned the other in our sights,
So in my brain the strong impression
Of thy rich labours worlds of thoughts created,
Which thoughts, being circumvolved in gyrelike motion,
Were spent with wonder as they were dilated,

Till giddy with amazement I fell down
In a deep trance. . . . When lo, to crown thy worth
I struggled with this passion that did drown
My abler faculties, and thus broke forth:
Palmer, thy travails well become thy name,
And thou in them shall live as long as fame.

(MODERNISED VERSION © G. GREER)

The Seasons

WILLIAM SHAKESPEARE

Spring versus Winter

When daisies pied, and violets blue,
   And lady-smocks all silver-white,
And cuckoo-buds of yellow hue
   Do paint the meadows with delight,
The cuckoo then, on every tree,
Mocks married men, for thus sings he,
     Cuckoo, cuckoo!
     O word of fear,
Unpleasing to a married ear!

When shepherds pipe on oaten straws,
   And merry larks are ploughmen's clocks,
When turtles tread, and rooks, and daws,
   And maidens bleach their summer smocks,
The cuckoo then, on every tree,
Mocks married men, for thus sings he,
     Cuckoo, cuckoo!
     O word of fear,
Unpleasing to a married ear!

When icicles hang by the wall,
   And Dick the shepherd blows his nail,
And Tom bears logs into the hall,
   And milk comes frozen home in pail,

When blood is nipped, and ways be foul,
Then nightly sings the staring owl,
    Th-wit to-who!
    A merry note,
While greasy Joan doth keel the pot.

When all around the wind doth blow,
   And coughing drowns the parson's saw,
And birds sit brooding in the snow,
   And Marian's nose looks red and raw,
When roasted crabs hiss in the bowl,
Then nightly sings the staring owl,
    Th-wit to-who!
    A merry note,
While greasy Joan doth keel the pot.

THOMAS HARDY

Weathers

I

THIS is the weather the cuckoo likes,
    And so do I;
When showers betumble the chestnut spikes,
    And nestlings fly:
And the little brown nightingale bills his best,
And they sit outside at 'The Travellers' Rest',
And maids come forth sprig-muslin drest,
And citizens dream of the south and west,
    And so do I.

II

This is the weather the shepherd shuns,
    And so do I;
When beeches drip in browns and duns,
    And thresh, and ply;
And hill-hid tides throb, throe on throe,
And meadow rivulets overflow,
And drops on gate-bars hang in a row,
And rooks in families homeward go,
    And so do I.

SAMUEL TAYLOR COLERIDGE

On Observing a Blossom on the First of February 1796

Sweet flower, that peeping from thy russet stem
Unfoldest timidly, (for in strange sort
This dark, frieze-coated, hoarse, teeth-chattering month
Hath borrowed Zephyr's voice, and gazed upon thee
With blue voluptuous eye), alas, poor Flower!
These are but flatteries of the faithless year.
Perchance, escaped its unknown polar cave,
Even now the keen North-East is on its way.
Flower that must perish! Shall I liken thee
To some sweet girl of too too rapid growth
Nipp'd by consumption mid untimely charms?
Or to Bristowa's bard, the wondrous boy!
An amaranth, which earth scarce seem'd to own,
Till disappointment came, and pelting wrong
Beat it to earth? Or with indignant grief
Shall I compare thee to poor Poland's hope,
Bright flower of hope killed in the opening bud?
Farewell, sweet blossom! Better fate be thine
And mock my boding! Dim similitudes
Weaving in moral strains, I've stolen one hour
From anxious Self, Life's cruel taskmaster!
And the warm wooings of this sunny day

Tremble along my frame and harmonise
The attempered organ, that even saddest thoughts
Mix with some sweet sensations, like harsh tunes
Played deftly on a soft-toned instrument.

PHILIP LARKIN

Coming

On longer evenings,
Light, chill and yellow,
Bathes the serene
Foreheads of houses.
A thrush sings,
Laurel-surrounded
In the deep bare garden,
Its fresh-peeled voice
Astonishing the brickwork.
It will be spring soon,
It will be spring soon –
And I, whose childhood
Is a forgotten boredom,
Feel like a child
Who comes on a scene
Of adult reconciling,
And can understand nothing
But the unusual laughter,
And starts to be happy.

THOMAS HARDY

A Backward Spring

THE trees are afraid to put forth buds,
And there is timidity in the grass;
The plots lie gray where gouged by spuds,
    And whether next week will pass
Free of sly sour winds is the fret of each bush
    Of barberry waiting to bloom.

Yet the snowdrop's face betrays no gloom,
And the primrose pants in its heedless push,
Though the myrtle asks if it's worth the fight
    This year with frost and rime
    To venture one more time
On delicate leaves and buttons of white
From the selfsame bough as at last year's prime,
And never to ruminate on or remember
What happened to it in mid-December.

ANON [SIR THOMAS BROWNE?]

Early Spring

The almond flourisheth, the birch-trees flow,
The sad mezereon cheerfully doth blow,
The flowery sons before their fathers seen.
The snails begin to crop the mandrake green;
The vernal sun with crocus gardens fills,
With hyacinths, anemones and daffodils.
The hazel catkins now dilate and fall,
And paronychions peep upon each wall.

(MODERNISED VERSION © G. GREER)

RICHARD WILBUR

April 5, 1974

The air was soft, the ground still cold.
In the dull pasture where I strolled
Was something I could not believe.
Dead grass appeared to slide and heave,
Though still too frozen-flat to stir,
And rocks to twitch, and all to blur.
What was this rippling of the land?
Was matter getting out of hand
And making free with natural law?
I stopped and blinked, and then I saw
A fact as eerie as a dream.
There was a subtle flood of steam
Moving upon the face of things.
It came from standing pools and springs
And what of snow was still around;
It came of winter's giving ground
So that the freeze was coming out,
As when a set mind, blessed by doubt,
Relaxes into mother-wit.
Flowers, I said, will come of it.

MURIEL SPARK

Complaint in a Wash-out Season

My mind's in pickle. Think of my talents all soused
in rainwater, April you All Fool's Month, you've doused
the light of your joke. Call off this protracted
intransigent deluge, it's hackneyed;
nothing to grizzle about now – winter's gone knock-kneed,
so turn off the tap,
you monstrous infant wetting Infinity's lap.
You turned the garden hose on;
you spat a million missiles aslant through a hundred dozen
long-range peashooters. You should be past
practical jokes in bad taste;
and what an old has-been you look when you flash
in the face of the sun in a shot-silk taffeta sash
and lift the petticoat clouds and dance a fandango.
You've rinsed the guaranteed colours out of the rainbow.
At least, when you wash your dye-streaked hair,
be so kind as to shake it out elsewhere,
and request the adenoidal firmament
not to sneeze all over my temperament.

E. E. CUMMINGS

'i thank You God for most this amazing ...'

i thank You God for most this amazing
day:for the leaping greenly spirits of trees
and a blue true dream of sky;and for everything
which is natural which is infinite which is yes

(i who have died am alive again today,
and this is the sun's birthday;this is the birth
day of life and of love and wings:and of the gay
great happening illimitably earth)

how should tasting touching hearing seeing
breathing any—lifted from the no
of all nothing—human merely being
doubt unimaginable You?

(now the ears of my ears awake and
now the eyes of my eyes are opened)

U. A. FANTHORPE

May 8th: how to recognise it

The tulips have finished their showy conversation.
Night's officers came briefly to report,
And took their heads off.

The limes have the look of someone
Who has been silent for a long time,
And is about to say a very good thing.

Roses grow taller, leafier,
Duller. They have star parts;
Like great actors, they hang about humbly in the wings.

On the lawn, daisies sustain their candid
Childish shout. Hippy dandelions are stoned
Out of their golden minds. And always

The rub-a-dub-dub recapitulation
Of grass blades growing. The plum tree is resting
Between blossom and fruit. Like a poker-player,

She doesn't show her hand. Daffodils
Are a matter of graceless brown leaves and rubber bands.
Wallflowers have turned bony.

This is not the shining childhood of spring,
But its homely adolescence, angular, hypothetical.
How one regrets the blue fingertips staggering
Up from the still dank earth.

ALFRED, LORD TENNYSON

Summer Night

Now sleeps the crimson petal, now the white;
　　Nor waves the cypress in the palace walk;
Nor winks the gold fin in the porphyry font:
The firefly wakens: waken thou with me.

　　Now droops the milk-white peacock like a ghost,
And like a ghost she glimmers on to me.

　　Now lies the Earth all Danaë to the stars,
And all thy heart lies open unto me.

　　Now slides the silent meteor on, and leaves
A shining furrow, as thy thoughts in me.

　　Now folds the lily all her sweetness up,
And slips into the bosom of the lake:
So fold thyself, my dearest, thou, and slip
Into my bosom and be lost in me.

HART CRANE

In Shadow

Out in the late amber afternoon,
Confused among chrysanthemums,
Her parasol, a pale balloon,
Like a waiting moon, in shadow swims.

Her furtive lace and misty hair
Over the garden dial distill
The sunlight, – then withdrawing, wear
Again the shadows at her will.

Gently yet suddenly, the sheen
Of stars inwraps her parasol.
She hears my step behind the green
Twilight, stiller than shadows, fall.

'Come, it is too late, – too late
To risk alone the light's decline:
Nor has the evening long to wait,' –
But her own words are night's and mine.

FREDEGOND SHOVE

Twilight in November

Rich chrysanthemums that drip
  Among the rusty palings. Brown
Burnished sheaf the frost must nip.
  Frost's a beggar to this town.

Sky that's as an eggshell green
  Merely glimmeringly known,
Since too lustrous to be seen
  Hidden like a jewel-stone.

Air as faint and pure as silk
  Lovelily and strangely freaked
All with mulberries in milk
  Stained and with fine orange streaked.

Bells the disembodied breath
  Of our fear and our belief,
Flying, flying after death,
  Dying with the sapless leaf.

Voices facing on the peace,
  Children's voices hoarse with zest,
A moon cut out of candle grease
  Waxing in the sunset's breast.

JENNY JOSEPH

The unlooked-for season

Love, the sun lies warm along the wall.
The wide windows and the smell of the road
Do not say 'Winter.' Ladybirds are crawling
Out on ledges. Midday full on the land
Slows down the progress of the afternoon
Promising evening, like a Summer Sunday.

But look where the sun is. Never high in the sky
It crept around the horizon. Ask anyone,
Look at the trees and the calendar – all declare
It should be Winter. Within two hours
The Winter night will come up with the fog.

Since you have come and gone in the dreaded season
And left so much in sunlight, I cannot think
Of now as a dead time, only gentle,
With nothing to be feared, if this is Winter.

STEWART CONN

Visiting Hour

In the pond of our new garden
were five orange stains, under
inches of ice. Weeks since anyone
had been there. Already by far
the most severe winter for years.
You broke the ice with a hammer.
I watched the goldfish appear,
blunt-nosed and delicately clear.

Since then so much has taken place
to distance us from what we were.
That it should come to this.
Unable to hide the horror
in my eyes, I stand helpless
by your bedside and can do no more
than wish it were simply a matter
of smashing the ice and giving you air.

ANNE RIDLER

Winter Poem

November smells of rue, bitter and musky,
Of mould, and fungus, and fog at the blue dusk.
The Church repents, and the trees, scattering their riches,
Stand up in bare bones.
But already the green buds sharpen for the first spring day,
Red embers glow on the twigs of the pyrus japonica,
And clematis awns, those burnished curly wigs,
Feather for the seeds' flight.

Stark Advent songs, the busy fungus of decay –
They are works of darkness that prepare the light,
And soon the candid frost lays bare all secrets.

The Gardener's Work

MATTHEW ARNOLD

Quiet Work

One lesson, Nature, let me learn of thee,
One lesson which with every wind is blown,
One lesson of two duties kept at one
Though the loud world proclaim their enmity –

Of toil unsevered from tranquillity!
Of labour, that in lasting fruit outgrows
Far noisier schemes, accomplished in repose,
Too great for haste, too high for rivalry!

Yes, while on earth a thousand discords ring,
Man's fitful uproar mingling with his toil,
Still do thy sleepless ministers move on,

Their glorious tasks in silence perfecting;
Still working, blaming still our vain turmoil,
Labourers that shall not fail, when man is gone.

FLEUR ADCOCK

Under the Lawn

It's hard to stay angry with a buttercup
threading through the turf (less and less a lawn
with each jagging rip of the fork or scoop
of the trowel) but a dandelion can

Inspire righteous fury: that taproot
drilling down to where it's impossible
ever quite to reach (although if it's cut
through that's merely a minor check) until

clunk: what's this? And it's spade-time. Several hours
later, eleven slabs of paving-stone
(submerged so long ago that the neighbours
who've been on the watch since 1941

'never remember seeing a path there') with,
lying marooned singly on three of them,
an octagonal threepence, a George the Fifth
penny and, vaguely missed from their last home

for fifteen years or so and rusted solid,
Grandpa's scissors, the ones for hairdressing
from his barbering days: plain steel, not plated;
still elegant; the tip of one blade still missing.

ROBERT FROST

Putting in the Seed

You come to fetch me from my work tonight
When supper's on the table, and we'll see
If I can leave off burying the white
Soft petals fallen from the apple tree
(Soft petals, yes, but not so barren quite,
Mingled with these, smooth bean and wrinkled pea),
And go along with you ere you lose sight
Of what you came for and become like me,
Slave to a springtime passion for the earth.
How Love burns through the Putting in the Seed
On through the watching for that early birth
When, just as the soil tarnishes with weed,
The sturdy seedling with arched body comes
Shouldering its way and shedding the earth crumbs.

EDWARD THOMAS

Sowing

It was a perfect day
For sowing; just
As sweet and dry was the ground
As tobacco-dust.

I tasted deep the hour
Between the far
Owl's chuckling first soft cry
And the first star.

A long stretched hour it was;
Nothing undone
Remained; the early seeds
All safely sown.

And now, hark at the rain,
Windless and light,
Half a kiss, half a tear,
Saying good-night.

DUNCAN BUSH

The Hook

I

I named it sickle. But he
uses it, the old man, and he called it:
the hook.

No longer new; a flatter curve
of blade than the gold on red: crescent
of an ellipse;

and implement, not emblem:
dull, rust oiled with usage; nicked, the
harshened silver edge.

But a tool perfects, almost
like nature, more stringent than art: millenia
winnowed to this

shape since Egypt was
the world's grainhouse, longer:
a moon-edge

cutting finer than a straight:
grass, not flesh: only the point would embed,
opening an enemy

like a full sack, or the edge hack
a limb, the swung first past its mark;
but savage enough

a symbol of agronomy
for rising serfs. The crossed hammer beat
this out blue once

in a man's fist; but mass
produced now for a dwindling few, this tool,
this weapon:

the steel flattened, arched, made
keen, even the white ash turned smooth, and
ferruled, by machine.

But finely weighted, this one:
light, as if I hefted only a handle, even
to the left hand,

sit learns the backsweep.
I stooped and swung; the wristy, ambidextral hook
slew grass,

forestroke and back. I think
no eye bought this, but wrist: by balanced weight,
like grain;

and that it is beautiful only
now, for the coarse use that refined it,
like the sea-stone.

2

Beautiful too is the word:
swathe. I laid low all afternoon tall, green,
slender seeded grasses

of more elegance than poplars.
Their stems fell sheaved after the stroke
like armfuls of bluebells,

the blade was wet with sap.
Doubled I stooped, climbing the field
all the hot afternoon

for these red stigmata,
skinned blisters on the mounts of
both white palms.

ROBERT FROST

The Objection to Being Stepped on

At the end of the row
I stepped on the toe
Of an unemployed hoe.
It rose in offense
And struck me a blow
In the seat of my sense.
It wasn't to blame
But I called it a name.
And I must say it dealt
Me a blow that I felt
Like a malice prepense.
You may call me a fool,
But was there a rule
The weapon should be
Turned into a tool?
And what do we see?
The first tool I step on
Turned into a weapon.

SEAMUS HEANEY

The Pitchfork

Of all implements, the pitchfork was the one
That came near to an imagined perfection:
When he tightened his raised hand and aimed with it,
It felt like a javelin, accurate and light.

So whether he played the warrior or the athlete
Or worked in earnest in the chaff and sweat,
He loved its grain of tapering, dark-flecked ash
Grown satiny from its own natural polish.

Riveted steel, turned timber, burnish, grain,
Smoothness, straightness, roundness, length and sheen.
Sweat-cured, sharpened, balanced, tested, fitted.
The springiness, the clip and dart of it.

And then when he thought of probes that reached the farthest,
He would see the shaft of a pitchfork sailing past
Evenly, imperturbably through space,
Its prongs starlit and absolutely soundless –

But has learned at last to follow that simple lead
Past its own aim, out to an other side
Where perfection – or nearness to it – is imagined
Not in the aiming but the opening hand.

WILLIAM EMPSON

Rolling the Lawn

You can't beat English lawns. Our final hope
Is flat despair. Each morning therefore ere
I greet the office, through the weekday air,
Holding the Holy Roller at the slope
(The English fetish, not the Texas Pope)
Hither and thither on my toes with care
I roll ours flatter and flatter. Long, in prayer,
I grub for daisies at whose roots I grope.

Roll not the abdominal wall; the walls of Troy
Lead, since a plumb-line ordered, could destroy.
Roll rather, where no mole dare sap, the lawn,
And ne'er his tumuli shall tomb your brawn.
World, roll yourself; and bear your roller, soul,
As martyrs gridirons, when God calls the roll.

PHILIP LARKIN

Cut Grass

Cut grass lies frail:
Brief is the breath
Mown stalks exhale.
Long, long the death

It dies in the white hours
Of young-leafed June
With chestnut flowers,
With hedges snowlike strewn,

White lilac bowed,
Lost lanes of Queen Anne's lace,
And that high-builded cloud
Moving at summer's pace.

ROBERT FROST

Gathering Leaves

Spades take up leaves
No better than spoons,
And bags full of leaves
Are light as balloons.

I make a great noise
Of rustling all day
Like rabbit and deer
Running away.

But the mountains I raise
Elude my embrace,
Flowing over my arms
And into my face.

I may load and unload
Again and again
Till I fill the whole shed,
And what have I then?

Next to nothing for weight;
And since they grew duller
From contact with earth,
Next to nothing for color.

Next to nothing for use.
But a crop is a crop,
And who's to say where
The harvest shall stop?

EDWARD THOMAS

Digging

Today I think
Only with scents, – scents dead leaves yield,
And bracken, and wild carrot's seed,
And the square mustard field;

Odours that rise
When the spade wounds the roots of tree,
Rose, currant, raspberry, or goutweed,
Rhubarb or celery;

The smoke's smell, too,
Flowing from where a bonfire burns
The dead, the waste, the dangerous,
And all to sweetness turns.

It is enough
To smell, to crumble the dark earth,
While the robin sings over again
Sad songs of Autumn mirth.

SEAMUS HEANEY

Digging

Between my finger and my thumb
The squat pen rests; snug as a gun.

Under my window, a clean rasping sound
When the space sinks into gravelly ground:
My father, digging. I look down

Till his straining rump among the flowerbeds
Bends low, comes up twenty years away
Stooping in rhythm through potato drills
Where he was digging.

The coarse boot nestled on the lug, the shaft
Against the inside knee was levered firmly.
He rooted out tall tops, buried the bright edge deep
To scatter new potatoes that we picked
Loving their cool hardness in our hands.

By God, the old man could handle a spade.
Just like his old man.

My grandfather cut more turf in a day
Than any other man on Toner's bog.
Once I carried him milk in a bottle

Corked sloppily with paper. He straightened up
To drink it, then fell to right away
Nicking and slicing neatly, heaving sods
Over his shoulder, going down and down
For the good turf. Digging.

The cold smell of potato mould, the squelch and slap
Of soggy peat, the curt cuts of an edge
Through living roots awaken in my head.
But I've no spade to follow men like them.

Between my finger and my thumb
The squat pen rests.
I'll dig with it.

MAXINE KUMIN

Turning the Garden in Middle Age

They have lain a long time, these two:
parsnip with his beard on his foot,
puddingstone with fool's gold in her ear
until, under the thrust of my fork,
earthlock lets go. Mineral
and marrow are flung loose in May
still clinging together as if
they had intended this embrace.

I think then of skulls picked clean
underground, and the long bones
of animals overturned in the woods
and the gorgeous insurgency
of these smart green weeds
erect now in every furrow
that lure me once more
to set seeds in the loam.

RUTH PITTER

The Morals of Pruning

When I, who stands as fate to this strong Vine,
Take up the steel, and the devoted shoot,
Not for its own felicity, but mine,
Eye sternly, and determined that the fruit
Is to be here and this, so much, no more –
I think of miseries that men deplore:

Their hopes curtailed, like the thinned cluster here:
Life interrupted, like this shortened stem;
Old certitudes removed, as when I shear
The gnarled unfruitful rods, and carry them
To the indifferent fire; such surgery
Life does upon my fellows, and on me.

If we could think our pain but part designed
By some such purpose as evokes this great
Delicious cluster, where we else should find
All wasteful and all trivial, then our fate
Might be absolved, and we more calmly grow;
At least they cannot prove it is not so.

THEODORE ROETHKE

Cuttings

Sticks-in-a-drowse droop over sugary loam,
Their intricate stem-fur dries;
But still the delicate slips keep coaxing up water;
The small cells bulge;

One nub of growth
Nudges a sand-crumb loose,
Pokes through a musty sheath
Its pale tendrilous horn.

Cuttings — (later)

This urge, wrestle, resurrection of dry sticks,
Cut stems struggling to put down feet,
What saint strained so much,
Rose on such lopped limbs to a new life?

I can hear, underground, that sucking and sobbing,
In my veins, in my bones I feel it, –
The small waters seeping upward,
The tight grains parting at last.

When sprouts break out,
Slippery as fish,
I quail, lean to beginnings, sheath-wet.

CAROL RUMENS

Weeds

In gardens, it's the unwanted
babies that grow best and biggest,
swarming our beds of frail
legitimate darlings with roots
like wire and crude, bright flower-heads.

They seem oblivious to the fury of steel prongs
earthquaking around them.
If they fall today, tomorrow
they'll stand all the greener.

Too soon, the beautiful lives
we've trembled over with sprays
of pesticide, friendly stakes,
and watering-cans at sunset,
give in, leaving us helpless.

The weeds, the unfavoured ones,
stare at us hungrily,
and since it is hard to live
empty of love, we try
to smile; we learn to forgive them.

WALTER DE LA MARE

A Widow's Weeds

A poor old Widow in her weeds
Sowed her garden with wild-flower seeds;
Not too shallow, and not too deep,
And down came April – drip – drip – drip.
Up shone May, like gold, and soon
Green as an arbour grew leafy June.
And now all summer she sits and sews
Where willow-herb, comfrey, bugloss blows,
Teasel and tansy, meadowsweet,
Campion, toadflax, and rough hawksbit;
Brown bee orchis, and Peals of Bells;
Clover, burnet, and thyme she smells;
Like Oberon's meadows her garden is
Drowsy from dawn till dusk with bees.
Weeps she never, but sometimes sighs,
And peeps at her garden with bright brown eyes;
And all she has is all she needs –
A poor old Widow in her weeds.

P. J. KAVANAGH

Elder

Feigns dead in winter, none lives better.
Chewed by cattle springs up stronger; an odd
Personal smell and unlovable skin;
Straight shoots like organ pipes in cigarette paper.
No nursery man would sell you an
Elder – 'not bush, not tree, not bad, not good'.
Judas was surely a fragile man
To hang himself from this – 'God's stinking tree'.

In summer juggles flower-plates in air,
Creamy as cumulus, and berries, each a weasel's eye
Of light. Pretends it's unburnable
(Who burns it sees the Devil), cringes, hides a soul
Of cream plates, purple fruits in a rattle
Of bones. A good example.

D. H. LAWRENCE

Leaves of Grass, Flowers of Grass

Leaves of grass, what about leaves of grass?
Grass blossoms, grass has flowers, flowers of grass
dusty pollen of grass, tall grass in its midsummer maleness,
hay-seed and tiny grain of grass, graminiferae
not far from the lily, the considerable lily;

even the blue-grass blossoms;
even the bison knew it;
even the stupidest farmer gathers his hay in bloom, in blossom
just before it seeds.

Only the best matters; even the cow knows it;
grass in blossom, blossoming grass, risen to its height and its
    natural pride
in its own splendour and its own feathery maleness
the grass, the grass.

Leaves of grass, what are leaves of grass, when at its best grass
    blossoms.

THEODORE ROETHKE

'Long Live the Weeds' — Hopkins

Long live the weeds that overwhelm
My narrow vegetable realm!
The bitter rock, the barren soil
That force the son of man to toil;
All things unholy, marred by curse,
The ugly of the universe.
The rough, the wicked, and the wild
That keep the spirit undefiled.
With these I match my little wit
And earn the right to stand or sit,
Hope, love, create, or drink and die:
These shape the creature that is I.

RUTH PITTER

The Tall Fruit-Trees

I'll lop them, it will be easier so to tend them;
    Then we may clean them and gather the fruit with ease;
    No one can do with these great old orchard trees,
Dirty, shady, unwieldy—don't try to defend them.

O promise to do them one or two at a time then—
    That will make you twenty years in going the rounds:
Then the tall tops for me will be out of bounds,
    Surely I shall no longer be able to climb then.

But while I am able O let me ascend the plum-tree
    And poke my head out at the top, where the lovely view
Has a foreground of scarlet plums with a wash of blue,
And I am away from earth in the starlings' country.

And for a few years yet spend a day in the pear-tree,
    Squirming and stretching, plagued by the wasps and the
        twigs,
Scratches all over me, bruised in the arms and legs,
    Coming down whacked at last from the great old bare
        tree—

And yet not wholly bare, for his topmost steeple
    Still flaunts a fair wreath of a dozen, the best of all;

Ha, he beat me at last, for he was so tall—
    He will not give his best work up to greedy people.

And there is the huge gaunt apple-tree, dead man's seedling,
    With five great limbs, spreading twenty feet from the
        ground;
How he makes us stagger the longest ladder around,
    So heavy—yet four feet short of the ladder we're needing.

Some years he's good for bushels of small red apples
    That keep well enough, and roast well enough by the fire,
But every year he is young and brave with desire,
    Smothered in rosy wreaths that the sunlight dapples.

Dappled with sunlight and bright with the May-time raindrop,
    Mighty from age and youthful with tender bloom,
He heaves up brightness and scent to our highest room,
    Brushes the dormer-window with shining maintop.

We'll take in a bit more ground, and plant it with limber
    Maidens on dwarfing stocks, at twelve feet apart;
But the great old trees are the real loves of my heart,
    Mountains of blossom and fruit on the stalwart timber.

JAMES FENTON

The Fruit-Grower in War-time (and some of his enemies)

These are the problems he inherits:
Bonfire rubbish has remained unburned for months,
Dry beech leaf is accumulating under
Beech hedges, those rotten peasticks have become
Cluttered up with autumn leaves and shrubberies
    Lie thick with excellent
    Weevil cover. Too late
For the administrator of Derris Dust
Since egg-laying is inside the bud. April,
He forewarned us, *is the weevil's busy month*
And the right time to employ that poison. If
    Only these weevils had been dusted

    In early Spring, *the hind legs* of the
Female *are said to be* affected, thus
Cramping her style at egg-laying. Precision
Counts for much, but foresight and provision are
Mandatory if total loss is to be
    Avoided. *Egg-laying . . .*
    Before the bud-cluster
Is beyond the green-bud stage. No poison will
Affect the hatched weevil, for it when feeding

114

On the leaf takes only the inner tissues
And it is small comfort to the fruit-grower
     To know that it sometimes disappears

     Almost as suddenly as it came.
He knows that what few apples survive attack
From weevils and mature have only to face
Further depredations from the sawfly and
Codling moth. Often, walking down orchard rows
     In summer where such pests
     Are prevalent, he has
Heard the sharp clicks as the innumerable
Apple-suckers jump from the apple leaves at
His approach, a pest whose winged generation
Can cloud the windscreens of bus-drivers in Kent.
     No wonder then that he cultivates

     Such minute accuracy. *Settling*
Herself at the edge of the calyx cup, where
Two sepals join, the sawfly faces into
The centre of the flower, ends her body down
And inserts her ovipositor into
     The side of the fruitlet.
     The eggs of the Codling
Moth are *noticeable only when the sun*
Glints on them. To control the grubs he will need
Not a single spray at petal fall (which is
Useless over a length of time) but a wash
     Between the 1st and 10th of July.

Add to this fast-growing list the two
Kinds of Capsid bug, *like a stream-lined aphis*
With wings and the ability to run fast,
Which *when seen on the leaf run round to the back,*
The Woolly Aphis called American Blight,
　　Which reproduces by
　　Parthenogenesis,
And caterpillars of the winter moth, *both*
Those which loop and those which wriggle hastily
Backwards. The resistance is numbered but now
Little remains save twisted leaves, brown wilted
Blossoms or dwarfed apples. Young branches

Festooned with white felty coverings . . .
Minute punctures with reddish margins spot the
Opening leaves . . . strange little dark lines and loops . . .
The appearance of the photos of the moon . . .
Dry seas and craters . . . a nasty sour smell where
　　Wet frass always exudes.
　　And for the future, one
Man stands between us and worse than this, his face
Kindly, his grey hairs venerable, and he
Knows what he is about. *Speak to him*, says his
Acquaintance, *at any time of the year and*
　　He'll either produce from a waistcoat

Pocket a tiny glass tube with the
Choicest bugs in it, or show you ever such
A beautiful portrait of one done of course

By himself. Such diligence. We find it hard,
Knowing that a bad harvest or a poor crop
    Can overthrow a state
    To overestimate
The value of his work. But something remains
Which gives us pause. We think of all those gallons
Of arsenate of lead being pumped over
Our native soil. How can we help comparing
    Ourselves to the last idiot heirs

    Of some Roman province, still for the
Sake of form eating off lead platters? With each
Bug destroyed and apple saved, we are nearer
Discovering what we are about. Meanwhile
We must observe the fruit-grower with caution
    But remember his friend's
    Stern charge that *it is you*
Who when you bite into an apple do not like to
Bite into a bug, that have led him into
His bloodthirsty way of life. One cannot doubt
That this is so and that in similar or
    Related cases, the paradigm holds true.

The Gardener's Companions

CHARLOTTE SMITH

To a green-chafer, on a white rose

You dwell within a lovely bower,
Little chafer, gold and green,
Nestling in the fairest flower,
The rose of snow, the garden's queen.

There you drink the chrystal dew,
And your shards* as emeralds bright
And corselet, of the ruby's hue,
Hide among the petals white.

Your fringèd feet may rest them there,
And there your filmy wings may close,
But do not wound the flower so fair
That shelters you in sweet repose.

Insect! be not like him who dares
On pity's bosom to intrude,
And then that gentle bosom tears
With baseness and ingratitude.

*shards. *Elytra*.

ANNA LAETITIA BARBAULD

The Caterpillar

No, helpless thing, I cannot harm thee now;
Depart in peace, thy little life is safe,
For I have scanned thy form with curious eye,
Noted the silver line that streaks thy back,
The azure and the orange that divide
Thy velvet sides; thee, houseless wanderer,
My garment has enfolded, and my arm
Felt the light pressure of thy hairy feet;

Thou hast curled round my finger; from its tip,
Precipitous descent! with stretched out neck,
Bending thy head in airy vacancy,
This way and that, inquiring, thou hast seemed
To ask protection; now, I cannot kill thee.
Yet I have sworn perdition to thy race,
And recent from the slaughter am I come
Of tribes and embryo nations: I have sought
With sharpened eye and persecuting zeal,
Where, folded in their silken webs they lay
Thriving and happy; swept them from the tree
And crushed whole families beneath my foot;
Or, sudden, poured on their devoted heads
The vials of destruction.—This I've done,
Nor felt the touch of pity: but when thou,—

A single wretch, escaped the general doom,
Making me feel and clearly recognise
Thine individual existence, life,
And fellowship of sense with all that breathes,—
Present'st thyself before me, I relent,
And cannot hurt thy weakness.—So the storm
Of horrid war, o'erwhelming cities, fields,
And peaceful villages, rolls dreadful on:
The victor shouts triumphant; he enjoys
The roar of cannon and the clang of arms,
And urges, by no soft relentings stopped,
The work of death and carnage. Yet should one,
A single sufferer from the field escaped,
Panting and pale, and bleeding at his feet,
Lift his imploring eyes,—the hero weeps;
He is grown human, and capricious Pity,
Which would not stir for thousands, melts for one
With sympathy spontaneous:—'Tis not Virtue,
Yet 'tis the weakness of a virtuous mind.

FLEUR ADCOCK

An Emblem

Someone has nailed a lucky horse-shoe
beside my door while I was out –
or is it a loop of rubber? No:
it's in two sections. They glide about,
silently undulating: two
slugs in a circle, tail to snout.

The ends link up: it's a shiny quoit
of rippling slug-flesh, thick as a snake,
liquorice-black against the white
paint; a pair of wetly-nak-
ed tubes. It doesn't seem quite right
to watch what kind of love they'll make.

But who could resist? I'll compromise
and give them a little time alone
to nuzzle each other, slide and ooze
into conjunction on their own;
surely they're experts, with such bodies,
each a complete erogenous zone –

self-lubricating, swelling smooth
and boneless under grainy skin.
Ten minutes, then, for them to writhe

in privacy, to slither in-
to position, to arrange each lithe
tapered hose-pipe around its twin.

All right, now, slugs, I'm back; time's up.
And what a pretty coupling I find!
They're swinging from the wall by a rope
of glue, spun out of their combined
mucus and anchored at the top.
It lets them dangle, intertwined,

formally perfect, like some emblem:
heraldic serpents coiled in a twist.
But just in case their pose may seem
immodest or exhibitionist
they've dressed themselves in a cloud of foam,
a frothy veil for love-in-a-mist.

THOM GUNN

Considering the Snail

The snail pushes through a green
night, for the grass is heavy
with water and meets over
the bright path he makes, where rain
has darkened the earth's dark. He
moves in a wood of desire,

pale antlers barely stirring
as he hunts. I cannot tell
what power is at work, drenched there
with purpose, knowing nothing.
What is a snail's fury? All
I think is that if later
I parted the blades above
the tunnel and saw the thin
trail of broken white across
litter, I would never have
imagined the slow passion
to that deliberate progress.

EMILY DICKINSON

Our little Kinsmen – after Rain
In plenty may be seen,
A Pink and Pulpy multitude
The tepid Ground upon.

A needless life, it seemed to me
Until a little Bird
As to a Hospitality
Advanced and breakfasted.

As I of He, so God of Me
I pondered, may have judged,
And left the little Angle Worm
With Modesties enlarged.

VICKI FEAVER

Glow Worm

Talking about the chemical changes
that make a body in love shine,
or even, for months, immune to illness,
you pick a grub from the lawn
and let it lie on your palm – glowing
like the emerald-burning butt
of a cigarette. (We still haven't touched,
only lain side by side
the half stories of our half lives.)
You call them lightning bugs
from the way the males gather in clouds
and simultaneously flash.
This is the female, fat from a diet
of liquefied snails, at the stage in her cycle
when she hardly eats; when all her energy's
directed to drawing water and oxygen
to a layer of luciferin.
Wingless, wordless,
in a flagrant and luminous bid
to resist the narrative's pull to death,
she lifts her shining green abdomen
to signal *yes yes yes*.

RICHARD FLECKNOE

The Ant

Little thinkest thou, poor ant, who there
  With so much toil and so much time
A grain or two to the cell dost bear,
  There's greater work in the world than thine.

In the small republic too at home,
  Where thou'rt perhaps some magistrate,
Little thinkest thou when thou dost come
  There's greater in the world than that.

Nor is it such wonder now in thee,
  No more of the world nor things dost know:
That all thy thoughts of the ground should be,
  And mind on things so poor and low.

But that man so base mind should bear
  To fix it on a clod of ground,
As there no greater business were,
  Nor greater worlds for to be found!

He so much of the man does want
  As metamorphosèd quite again;
Whilst thou'rt but man turned grovelling ant:
  Such grovellers seem but ants turned men.

WILLIAM EMPSON

The Ants

We tunnel through your noonday out to you.
We carry our tube's narrow darkness there
Where, nostrum-plastered, with prepared air,
With old men running and trains whining through

We ants may tap your aphids for your dew.
You may not wish their sucking or our care;
Our all-but freedom, too, your branch must bear,
High as roots' depth in earth, all earth to view.

No, by too much this station the air nears.
How small a chink lets in how dire a foe.
What though the garden in one glance appears?

Winter will come and all her leaves will go.
We do not know what skeleton endures.
Carry at least her parasites below.

DAVID CONSTANTINE

The Wasps

The apples on the tree are full of wasps;
Red apples, racing like hearts. The summer pushes
Her tongue into the winter's throat.

But at six today, like rain, like the first drops,
The wasps came battering softly at the black glass.
They want the light, the cold is at their backs.

That morning last year when the light had been left on
The strange room terrified the heart in me,
I could not place myself, didn't know my own

Insect scribble: then saw the whole soft
Pelt of wasps, its underbelly, the long black pane
Yellow with visitants, it seethed, the glass sounded.

I bless my life: that so much wants in.

EMILY DICKINSON

Like Trains of Cars on Tracks of Plush
I hear the level Bee –
A Jar across the Flowers goes
Their Velvet Masonry

Withstands until the sweet Assault
Their Chivalry consumes –
While He, victorious tilts away
To vanquish other Blooms.

ELIZABETH JENNINGS

The Ladybird's Story

It was a roadway to me.
So many meeting-places and directions.
It was smooth, polished, sometimes it shook a little
But I did not tumble off.
I heard you say, and it was like a siren,
'A ladybird. Good luck. Perhaps some money.'
I did not understand.
Suddenly I was frightened, fearful of falling
Because you lifted your hand.

And then I saw your eyes,
Glassy moons always changing shape,
Sometimes suns in eclipse.
I watched the beak, the peak of your huge nose
And the island of your lips.
I was afraid but you were not. I have
No sting. I do not wound.
I carry a brittle coat. It does not protect.
I thought you would blow me away but superstition
Saved me. You held your hand now in one position.
Gentled me over the veins and arteries.
But it was not I you cared about but money.
You see I have watched you with flies.

PAUL MULDOON

Hedgehog

The snail moves like a
Hovercraft, held up by a
Rubber cushion of itself,
Sharing its secret

With the hedgehog. The hedgehog
Shares its secret with no one.
We say, *Hedgehog, come out
Of yourself and we will love you.*

*We mean no harm. We want
Only to listen to what
You have to say. We want
Your answers to our questions.*

The hedgehog gives nothing
Away, keeping itself to itself.
We wonder what a hedgehog
Has to hide, why it so distrusts.

We forget the god
Under this crown of thorns.
We forget that never again
Will a god trust in the world.

PHILIP LARKIN

The Mower

The mower stalled, twice; kneeling, I found
A hedgehog jammed up against the blades,
Killed. It had been in the long grass.

I had seen it before, and even fed it, once.
Now I had mauled its unobtrusive world
Unmendably. Burial was no help:

Next morning I got up and it did not.
The first day after a death, the new absence
Is always the same; we should be careful

Of each other, we should be kind
While there is still time.

SYLVIA PLATH

Blue Moles

I

They're out of the dark's ragbag, these two
Moles dead in the pebbled rut,
Shapeless as flung gloves, a few feet apart—
Blue suede a dog or fox has chewed.
One, by himself, seemed pitiable enough,
Little victim unearthed by some large creature
From his orbit under the elm root.
The second carcase makes a duel of the affair:
Blind twins bitten by bad nature.

The sky's far dome is sane and clear.
Leaves, undoing their yellow caves
Between the road and the lake water,
Bare no sinister spaces. Already
The moles look neutral as the stones.
Their corkscrew noses, their white hands
Uplifted, stiffen in a family prose.
Difficult to imagine how fury struck—
Dissolved now, smoke of an old war.

2

Nightly the battle-shouts start up
In the ear of the veteran, and again
I enter the soft pelt of the mole.
Light's death to them: they shrivel in it.
They move through their mute rooms while I sleep,
Palming the earth aside, grubbers
After the fat children of root and rock,
By day, only the topsoil heaves.
Down there one is alone.

Outsize hands prepare a path,
They go before: opening the veins,
Delving for the appendages
Of beetles, sweetbreads, shards – to be eaten
Over and over. And still the heaven
Of final surfeit is just as far
From the door as ever. What happens between us
Happens in darkness, vanishes
Easy and often as each breath.

EMILY DICKINSON

Within my Garden, rides a Bird
Upon a single Wheel –
Whose spokes a dizzy Music make
As 'twere a travelling Mill –

He never stops, but slackens
Above the Ripest Rose –
Partakes without alighting
And praises as he goes,

Till every spice is tasted –
And then his Fairy Gig
Reels in remoter atmospheres –
And I rejoin my Dog,

And He and I, perplex us
If positive, 'twere we –

Or bore the Garden in the Brain
This Curiosity –

But He, the best Logician,
Refers my clumsy eye –
To just vibrating Blossoms!
An Exquisite Reply!

PHOEBE HESKETH

Blue Tits

Bobbing on willow branches, blue and yellow,
Acrobatic blue tits swing and sway
In careful somersaults and neat gyrations
Grub-picking deftly down each bending spray.

Now one rebuffs an alien intruder –
Humdrum sparrow, drab among the gold –
Churrs and scolds in azure-crested anger,
Scuttles down a twig in blue and bold
Defiance at this urchin gutter-haunter
Till all the blues combine against one grey:
Active whirr and flutter, feathered thunder
Of tiny wings to drive the foe away.

Brave blue tit, white-cheeked like a painted toy
Jerking to life from pavement-seller's string,
Twirls round twigs, his natural trapezes,
Darts to snap a moth upon the wing.
Plumb-as-willow-catkin, primrose-breasted,
This sky-capped morsel magnifies the Spring.

ANONYMOUS

The Blackbird

In midst of woods or pleasant grove
    Where all sweet birds do sing,
Methought I heard so rare a sound,
    Which made the heavens to ring.
The charm was good, the noise full sweet,
    Each bird did play his part;
And I admired to hear the same;
    Joy sprung into my heart.

The blackbird made the sweetest sound,
    Whose tunes did far excel,
Full pleasantly and most profound
    Was all things placèd well.
Thy pretty tune, mine own sweet bird,
    Done with so good a grace,
Extols thy name, prefers the same
    Abroad in every place.

Thy music grave, bedeckèd well
    With sundry points of skill,
Bewrays thy knowledge excellent,
    Engrafted in thy will.
My tongue shall speak, my pen shall write,
    In praise of thee to tell.
The sweetest bird that ever was,
    In friendly sort, farewell.

R. S. THOMAS

Swifts

The swifts winnow the air.
It is pleasant at the end of the day
To watch them. I have shut the mind
On fools. The 'phone's frenzy
Is over. There is only the swifts'
Restlessness in the sky
And their shrill squealing.
　Sometimes they glide,
Or rip the silk of the wind
In passing. Unseen ribbons
Are trailing upon the air.
There is no solving the problem
They pose, that had millions of years
Behind it, when the first thinker
Looked at them.
　Sometimes they meet
In the high air; what is engendered
At contact? I am learning to bring
Only my wonder to the contemplation
Of the geometry of their dark wings.

GRACE TOLLEMACHE

The Swallow's Note

The swallow's cry that's so forlorn,
    By thrush and blackbird overpowered,
Is like the hidden thorn
    On the rose-bush, deep-bowered:

But when the song of every bird
    Is hushed, in Summer's lull profound,
And all alone is heard
Its little poignant sound,

The piteous shrill of its sharp grief
    Seems, in the silence of the air,
The thorn, without a leaf,
    On the wild rose-bush, bare!

The Gardener's Machinations

ANDREW MARVELL

The Mower against Gardens

Luxurious man, to bring his vice in use,
    Did after him the world seduce,
And from the fields the flowers and plants allure
    Where Nature was most plain and pure.
He first enclosed within the garden's square
    A still and standing pool of air,
And a more luscious earth for them did knead
    Which stupefied them as it fed.
The pink grew then as double as his mind;
    The nutriment did change the kind.
With strange perfumes he did the roses taint,
    And flowers themselves were taught to paint.
The tulip, white, did for complexion seek
    And learnt to interline its cheek;
Its onion root they then so high did hold
    That one was for a meadow sold.
Another world was searched through oceans new
    To find the Marvel of Peru.
And yet these rarities might be allowed
    To man, that sovereign thing and proud,
Had he not dealt between the bark and tree,
    Forbidden mixtures there to see.
No plant now knew the stock from whence it came.
    He grafts upon the wild the tame,

That the uncertain and adulterate fruit
    Might put the palate in dispute.
His green seraglio has its eunuchs too,
    Lest any tyrant him out-do,
And in the cherry, he does Nature vex,
    To procreate without a sex.
'Tis all enforced, the fountain and the grot,
    While the sweet fields do lie forgot,
Where willing Nature does to all dispense
    A wild and fragrant innocence,
And fauns and fairies do the meadows till
    More by their presence than their skill.
Their statues polished by some ancient hand
    May to adorn the gardens stand,
But, howsoe'er the figures excel,
    The gods themselves with us do dwell.

(MODERNISED VERSION © G. GREER)

SIMON ARMITAGE

Greenhouse

It's gone to seed now; each loose pane pitted
with lichen like the walls of a fish tank,
the soffits lagged with a fur of cobwebs.
I burst in the other day; kicked the door
out of its warped frame, stood in the green light
among nine years of unnatural growth
and thought back to the morning we built it.
We used the old sash windows from the house,
held them flat with leather gloves, steadied them
down the path. I remember that journey:
you out in front, unsure of your footing
on the damp stones, and me behind counting
each of your steps through our cargo of glass.

Some nights I'd watch from my bedroom window
as you arrived home late from a concert,
and leaving the headlights on to guide you
waded into the black of the garden.
I'd wait, straining for the sound of the hasp
or guessing your distance by the sparkle
of a cufflink. When you disturbed them
the seeds of rose-bay willow-herbs lifted
like air bubbles into the beam of light.

Then you'd emerge, a hoard of tomatoes
swelling the lap of your luminous shirt;
and caught in the blur of double glazing
your perfect ghost, just one step behind you.

WILLIAM COWPER

The Pine-Apple and the Bee

THE pine-apples, in triple row,
Were basking hot, and all in blow;
A bee of most discerning taste
Perceived the fragrance as he passed,
On eager wing the spoiler came,
And search'd for crannies in the frame,
Urged his attempt on every side,
To every pane his trunk applied;
But still in vain, the frame was tight,
And only pervious to the light:
Thus having wasted half the day,
He trimmed his flight another way.
   Methinks, I said, in thee I find
The sin and madness of mankind.
To joys forbidden man aspires,
Consumes his soul with vain desires;
Folly the spring of his pursuit,
And disappointment all the fruit.
While Cynthio ogles, as she passes,
The nymph between two chariot glasses,
She is the pineapple, and he
The silly unsuccessful bee.
The maid who views with pensive air
The show-glass fraught with glittering ware,

Sees watches, bracelets, rings, and lockets,
But sighs at thought of empty pockets;
Like thine, her appetite is keen,
But ah, the cruel glass between!

Our dear delights are often such,
Exposed to view, but not to touch;
The sight our foolish heart inflames,
We long for pine-apples in frames;
With hopeless wish one looks and lingers;
One breaks the glass, and cuts his fingers;
But they whom truth and wisdom lead
Can gather honey from a weed.

FREDA DOWNIE

Ferns

The ferns in the lean-to conservatory dissolved light,
Made you feel you were pushing around under water
Or still wearing your green summer eye-shade.
They drifted on whitened shelving from pots
Decorated with ruched crêpe papers – and one fern
Stood in a fluted container someone had fashioned
From an old gramophone record of black shellac.

They clouded out the glazed slope of sooty sky,
Curtained the dining-room window with filmy green
So that in the house too, you wavered in a marine wash,
Spoke slow-mouthed to the woman with fronded hands
Or woke, like Yadwigha, on the chaise-longue of red plush
Still dreaming the jungle hung silently at your back –
Until someone put on the light and moved about.

THOMAS HARDY

The Frozen Greenhouse — (St Juliot)

'THERE was a frost
Last night!' she said,
'And the stove was forgot
When we went to bed,
And the greenhouse plants
Are frozen dead!'

By the breakfast blaze
Blank-faced spoke she,
Her scared young look
Seeming to be
The very symbol
Of tragedy.

The frost is fiercer
Than then to-day,
As I pass the place
Of her once dismay,
But the greenhouse stands
Warm, tight, and gay,

While she who grieved
At the sad lot
Of her pretty plants —

Cold, iced, forgot –
Herself is colder,
And knows it not.

ROBERT GRAVES

The Florist Rose

This wax-mannequin nude, the florist rose,
She of the long stem and too glossy leaf,
Is dead to honest greenfly and leaf-cutter:
Behind plate-glass watches the yellow fogs.

Claims kin with the robust male aeroplane
Whom eagles hate and phantoms of the air,
Who has no legend, as she breaks from legend—
From fellowship with sword and sail and crown.

Experiment's flower, scentless (he its bird);
Is dewed by the spray-gun; is tender-thorned;
Pouts, false-virginal, between bud and bloom;
Bought as a love-gift, droops within the day.

AMY CLAMPITT

High Culture

The geranium and the begonia
bloom with such offhand redundance
we scarcely notice. But the
amaryllis is a study in

disruption: everything routine
gives way to the unsheathing
of its climbing telescope—
a supernova of twin crimson

tunnels, porches of infinity
where last week there was nothing.
Months of clandestine preparation
now implode in pollen

that will never brush a bee,
fueling the double-barreled velvet
stairwell of its sterile pistils
with a tapered incandescence

that's already short of breath
and going blind before a
week is out. Such show
of breeding, such an excess

of cultivation, all but asks us
to stop breathing too until
it's over. I remember
how, the night the somewhat

famous violinist came to supper,
the whisper of the gown she
put on just before the concert
filled the parlor of the farmhouse

with things it had no room for—
the slave marts of the East,
the modes of Paris, the gazing
ramparts of the stratosphere.

LOUIS MACNEICE

Flower Show

Marooned by night in a canvas cathedral under bare bulbs
He plods the endless aisles not daring to close an eye
To massed brass bands of flowers; these flowers are not to pluck
Which (cream cheese, paper, glass, all manner of textile and
    plastic)
Having long since forgotten, if they ever knew, the sky
Are grown, being forced, uprooted.

Squidlike, phallic or vulvar, hypnotic, idiotic, oleaginous,
Fanged or whaleboned, wattled or balding, brimstone or cold
As trout or seaweed, these blooms, ogling or baneful, all
Keep him in their blind sights; he tries to stare them down
But they are too many, too unreal, their aims are one, the
    controlled
Aim of a firing party.

So bandaged his eyes since he paid to come in but somehow
    forgot
To follow the others out – and now there is no way out
Except that his inturned eyes before he falls may show him
Some nettled orchard, tousled hedge, some garden even
Where flowers, whether they boast or insinuate, whisper or
    shout,
Still speak a living language.

MEDBH MCGUCKIAN

Gentians

In my alpine house, the slavery I pay
My wilful gentians! exploring all their pleats
And tucks as though they had something precious
Deep inside, that beard of camel-hair
In the throat. I watch them
Ease their heads so slowly
Through their thumbhole necklines, till they sit
Like tailors in their earth shoes,
Their watery husbands' knots. No insects
Visit them, nor do their ovaries swell,
Yet every night in Tibet their seeds
Are membraned by the snow, their roots
Are bathed by the passage of melt-water;
They tease like sullen spinsters
The dewfall of summer limes.

RUTH PITTER

Pot-bound

O I am root-bound! In this earthen Pot
How many a strangling noose and writhing knot
Describe contorted misery! a tomb
Where one woe for another leaves not room!
A charnel-house of starved desires, whence all
Is gone of Humus and good Mineral,
Or anything on which a Plant might feed
Till it could blossom and produce a seed;
Where wretched Worms, to their own hurt, have got
In by mischance, and poison all the pot:
Where the poor roots, for want of object fit,
Embrace the Drainage-crock, make much of it,
And glide, and feel, and search all ways in vain,
Sick for the Food and Space they can't attain,
And to the pining Branches only send
A negative, a warning of the End;
For if a growing Plant's not potted-on,
Betimes, and given new soil, its hope is gone.

O Gardener (if Gardener there be)
Behold this yellow leaf, and succour me!
From wizened stem and flowerless twig infer
The panic of the roots, whose silent stir
If rendered vocal, would affront the sky

With a great Mob's most hoarse and dreadful cry!
O tap me out! The tangled mass uncoil,
And rid my root of the exhausted soil!
Prod, O prod forth the unlucky Worms, and send
Them where they serve a salutary end;
The close-invested Drainage-crock pluck out,
Which the starved filaments have meshed about;
Spread out their aching toils, and then, O then,
Enlarge me into a clean Number Ten,
With some sweet rotted Turf, some crumbling Loam,
That I may feel myself at last at home,
And bud, and flourish, finally to be
A credit to my kind, and unto thee!
A long-retarded Plant, when thus relieved,
May grow so swiftly, and so thickly leaved
And richly budded, that its bright Ascent
And Blossoming are an Astonishment:
O give me leave thus to aspire and blow,
And come at last to the great Flower-show,
Where every past Despair and bygone Grief
I'll sublimate in each transcendent Leaf;
The bitter darkness of that former gloom
Will write in all the brilliance of a Bloom;
The absence of the Worm will celebrate
In Perfume worthy of an Emperor's state;
That all may say, 'Why, here's a Flower indeed!'
And crave a Slip of me, or else a Seed.

ALICE OSWALD

The Melon Grower

She concerned him,
but the connection had come loose.
They made shift with tiffs and silence.

He sowed a melon seed.
He whistled in the greenhouse.
She threw a slipper at him

and something jostled in the loam
as if himself had been layed blind.
She misperceived him. It rained.

The melon got eight leaves, it lolled.
She banged the plates.
He considered his fretful webby hands.

'If I can sex' he said 'the flowers,
very gently I'll touch their parts
with a pollen brush made of rabbit hairs.'

The carpels swelled. He had to prop them on pots.
She wanted the house repainting.
He was out the back watering.

He went to church, he sang 'O Lord how long shall the
    wicked . . .?'
He prayed, with his thumbs on his eyes.
His head, like a melon, pressured his fingers.

The shoots lengthened
and summer mornings came with giant shadows
and arcs as in the interim of a resurrection.

She stayed in bed, she was coughing.
He led the side-shoots along the wires.
She threw the entire tea-trolley downstairs.

And when the milk was off
and when his car had two flat tyres
and when his daughter left saying she'd had enough,

he was up a ladder hanging soft nets from the beam
to stop the fruit so labouring the stem.
The four globes grew big at ease

and a melony smell filled the whole place
and he caught her once, confused in the greenhouse,
looking for binder-twine. Or so she says.

THEODORE ROETHKE

Transplanting

Watching hands transplanting,
Turning and tamping,
Lifting the young plants with two fingers,
Sifting in a palm-full of fresh loam,—
One swift movement,—
Then plumping in the bunched roots,
A single twist of the thumbs, a tamping and turning,
All in one,
Quick on the wooden bench,
A shaking down, while the stem stays straight,
Once, twice, and a faint third thump,—
Into the flat-box it goes,
Ready for the long days under the sloped glass:

The sun warming the fine loam,
The young horns winding and unwinding,
Creaking their thin spines,
The underleaves, the smallest buds
Breaking into nakedness,
The blossoms extending
Out into the sweet air,
The whole flower extending outward,
Stretching and reaching.

KATHLEEN RAINE

The Trees in Tubs

Little laurel trees, your roots can find
No mountain, yet your leaves extend
Beyond your own world into mine
Perennial wands, unfolding in my thought
The budding evergreen of time.

ANNE RIDLER

Azalea in the House

This little shabby tree, forgotten all summer,
And crouched in its corner through December frost,
Now is brought indoors to keep its promise.
It speaks in a blaze, like a prophet returned from the wilderness:
The buds throw off their brown extinguishers, burst
Into flame, and March sees a midsummer feast.

Explosion of sunsets, archangels on a needle-point,
Red parliament of butterflies . . .
I cannot hold it with words, yet summer life
While winter howls out there behind the glass
And trees still clench their fists, must be too brief.

Scentless, infertile, kept from moth and rain,
Colour is its whole theme,
Like those vermilion rose-trees that bloom
In picture-books. They never drooped or faded,
But this has only a short month to shine,
And hours not spent in watching it are wasted.

WILLIAM COWPER

Inscription for a Moss-house in the Shrubbery at Weston

Here, free from riot's hated noise,
Be mine, ye calmer, purer joys,
    A book or friend bestows;
Far from the storms that shake the great,
Contentment's gale shall fan my seat,
    And sweeten my repose.

The Gardener's Reward

IVOR GURNEY

The Garden

The ordered curly and plain cabbages
Are all set out like school-children in rows;
In six short weeks shall these no longer please,
For with that ink-proud lady the rose, pleasure goes.

I cannot think what moved the poet men
So to write panegyrics of that foolish
Simpleton – while wild rose as fresh again
Lives, and the drowsed cabbages keep soil coolish.

KATHERINE PIERPOINT

The Dreaming Bean

This is the germinal spot of gathering green.
A close-curled, blissful fist
Of dreaming bean, milk-wet opal in the pod.

Held in the damp, white hollow of down,
The touch of light sifts through slim walls of sap
Circling, drifting cool and fine, to a whispertip.

A juicebubble; single, wetblown membrane,
Sphere of spun water, held high to the sun
In convergent slipstreams of light and air.

Not yet a thing of earth, the bean lies curled and
Swelling into itself, welling like a favourite thought.
Its stem is a pointing finger, to focus colour, meaning and
    delight.

The stem refines, and then instils a greater world;
A gathering up and soundless pouring into a quiet green
    pool.
A flow of growing vision into the beholding eye.

The pod moves – small wimple, turning on the breeze –
And steadies again. The dreaming bean

Makes the slightest of slipping squeaks against the skin
Like a wet finger on the boat's white hull.

A drop of breathing seasound in the sappy shell,
Starting to dream of changing state,
Of firming the sap to smoothness,
Of forming two soft, mirrorlinked halves;
This bean, the young old milk-tooth of the earth.

CHARLES TOMLINSON

Parsnips — For Ted Chamberlin

A mixed crop. I dig a clump:
Crotches seamed with soil,
Soil clinging to every hair,
To excrescences and mandrake mandibles.
Poor bare forked earth-stained animals,
One comes up whole and white,
A vegetable Adam. I take the lot
And wash them at the stream.
Rubbing, rinsing, I let fall
Inevitably this image of perfection,
Then rush for a garden rake
To fish it back again and run
Trying to out-race the current's
Rain-fed effervescence:
Fit image of the poet, he
In the waterproof, with the iron comb who goes
Hunting a prey that's halfway to the sea.

EDWARD THOMAS

Swedes

They have taken the gable from the roof of clay
On the long swede pile. They have let in the sun
To the white and gold and purple of curled fronds
Unsunned. It is a sight more tender-gorgeous
At the wood-corner where Winter moans and drips
Than when, in the Valley of the Tombs of Kings,
A boy crawls down into a Pharaoh's tomb
And, first of Christian men, beholds the mummy,
God and monkey, chariot and throne and vase,
Blue pottery, alabaster, and gold.

But dreamless long-dead Amen-hotep lies.
This is a dream of Winter, sweet as Spring.

ALEXANDER POPE

The Gardens of Alcinous

From the Seventh Book of Homer's Odyssey

Close to the gates a spacious garden lies,
From storms defended, and inclement skies:
Four acres was th' allotted space of ground,
Fenced with a green enclosure all around.
Tall thriving trees confess'd the fruitful mould;
The reddening apple ripens here to gold,
Here the blue fig with luscious juice o'erflows,
With deeper red the full pomegranate glows,
The branch here bends beneath the weighty pear,
And verdant olives flourish round the year.
The balmy spirit of the western gale
Eternal breathes on fruits untaught to fail:
Each dropping pear a following pear supplies,
On apples apples, figs on figs arise:
The same mild season gives the blooms to blow,
The buds to harden, and the fruits to grow.
Here ordered vines in equal ranks appear
With all the united labours of the year,
Some to unload the fertile branches run,
Some dry the blackening clusters in the sun,
Others to tread the liquid harvest join,
The groaning presses foam with floods of wine.

Here are the vines in early flower descried,
Here grapes discolour'd on the sunny side,
And there in autumn's richest purple dyed.
Beds of all various herbs, for ever green,
In beauteous order terminate the scene.
Two plenteous fountains the whole prospect crowned;
This through the gardens leads its streams around,
Visits each plant, and waters all the ground:
While that in pipes beneath the palace flows,
And thence its current on the town bestows;
To various use their various streams they bring,
The people one, and one supplies the king.

(MODERNISED VERSION © G. GREER)

ROBERT FROST

After Apple-picking

My long two-pointed ladder's sticking through a tree
Toward heaven still,
And there's a barrel that I didn't fill
Beside it, and there may be two or three
Apples I didn't pick upon some bough.
But I am done with apple-picking now.
Essence of winter sleep is on the night,
The scent of apples: I am drowsing off.
I cannot rub the strangeness from my sight
I got from looking through a pane of glass
I skimmed this morning from the drinking trough
And held against the world of hoary grass.
It melted, and I let it fall and break.
But I was well
Upon my way to sleep before it fell,
And I could tell
What form my dreaming was about to take.
Magnified apples appear and disappear,
Stem end and blossom end,
And every fleck of russet showing clear.
My instep arch not only keeps the ache,
It keeps the pressure of a ladder-round.
I feel the ladder sway as the boughs bend.
And I keep hearing from the cellar bin

The rumbling sound
Of load on load of apples coming in.
For I have had too much
Of apple-picking: I am overtired.
Of the great harvest I myself desired.
There were ten thousand thousand fruit to touch,
Cherish in hand, lift down, and not let fall.
For all
That struck the earth,
No matter if not bruised or spiked with stubble,
Went surely to the cider-apple heap
As of no worth.
One can see what will trouble
This sleep of mine, whatever sleep it is.
Were he not gone,
The woodchuck could say whether it's like his
Long sleep, as I describe its coming on,
Or just some human sleep.

U. A. FANTHORPE

Pomona and Vertumnus

Lady of kitchen-gardens, learned
In the ways of the early thin-skinned rhubarb,
Whose fingers fondle each gooseberry bristle,
Stout currants sagging on their flimsy stalks,
And sprinting strawberries, that colonize
As quick as Rome.

Goddess of verges, whose methodical
Tenderness fosters the vagrant croppers,
Gawky raspberry refugees from gardens,
Hip, sloe, juniper, blackberry, crab,
Humble abundance of heath, hedge, copse,
The layabouts' harvest.

Patron of orchards, pedantic observer
Of rites, of prune, graft, spray and pick,
In whose honour the Bramley's branches
Bow with their burly cargo, from grass-deep
To beyond ladders; you who teach pears their proper shape,
And brush the ripe plum's tip with a touch of crystal.

I know your lovers, earth's grubby godlings:
Silvanus, whose province is muck-heaps
And electric fences; yaffle-headed Picus;

Faunus the goatman. All of them friends
Of the mud-caked cattle, courting you gruffly
With awkward, touching gifts.

But I am the irrepressible, irresponsible
Spirit of Now: no constant past,
No predictable future. All my genius
Goes into moments. I have nothing to give
But contradiction and alteration.

ANNE RIDLER

Picking Pears

Nor heaven, nor earth, a state between,
    Whose walls of leaves
Weave in a chequer of dark and bright
The falling sky; whose roofs of green
Are held by ropes and chains and beams of light.

Regenerate summer hangs in the trees:
    Hours of sunshine
    Charged the cells, and spread the loot
So thick about us that we seize
    Even the leaves dissembling globes of fruit.

Strange that we only in harvest season
    Borrow from birds
    These parks of air, these visions over the fence:
Not the flat view of soaring reason
    But a sharper angle, the height of exalted sense.

We enter only to despoil:
    Solaced and proud
Though a barren twigs are left behind,
Through a weft of leaves we sink to the soil,
But summer's nimbus shrivels on the rind.

ANACREONTEA 55

The Rose

While we invoke the wreathèd spring,
Resplendent rose! to thee we'll sing;
Resplendent rose! The flower of flowers,
Whose breath perfumes Olympus' bowers;
Whose virgin blush, of chastened dye,
Enchants so much our mortal eye.
When Pleasure's bloomy season glows,
The Graces love to twine the rose;
The rose is warm Dione's bliss,
It flushes like Dione's kiss!
Oft has the poet's magic tongue
The rose's fair luxuriance sung;
And long the Muses, heavenly maids,
Have reared it in their tuneful shades.
When, at the early glance of morn,
It sleeps upon the glittering thorn,
'Tis sweet to dare the tangled fence,
To cull the timid floweret thence,
And wipe, with tender hand, away
The tear that on its blushes lay!
'Tis sweet to hold the infant stems,
Yet dropping with Aurora's gems,
And fresh inhale the spicy sighs
That from the weeping buds arise.

When revel reigns, when mirth is high,
And Bacchus beams in every eye,
Our rosy fillets scent exhale,
And fill with balm the fainting gale!
Oh, there is nought in nature bright,
Where roses do not shed their light!
When morning paints the orient skies,
Her fingers burn with roseate dyes;
The nymphs display the rose's charms,
It mantles o'er their graceful arms;
Through Cytherea's form it glows,
And mingles with the living snows.
The rose distils a healing balm,
The beating pulse of pain to calm;
Preserves the cold inurnèd clay,
And mocks the vestige of decay:
And when at length, in pale decline,
Its florid beauties fade and pine,
Sweet as in youth, its balmy breath
Diffuses odour e'en in death!
Oh! whence could such a plant have sprung?
Attend – for thus the tale is sung.
When humid, from the silvery stream
Effusing beauty's warmest beam,
Venus appeared in flushing hues,
Mellowed by Ocean's briny dews;
When, in the starry courts above,
The pregnant brain of mighty Jove
Disclosed the nymph of azure glance,

The nymph who shakes the martial lance!
Then, then, in strange eventful hour,
The earth produced an infant flower,
Which sprung, with blushing tinctures dressed,
And wantoned o'er its parent breast.
The gods beheld this brilliant birth,
And hailed the Rose, the boon of earth!
With nectar drops, a ruby tide,
The sweetly orient buds they dyed,
And bade them bloom, the flowers divine,
Of him who sheds the teeming vine;
And bade them on the spangled thorn,
Expand their bosoms to the morn.

TRANSLATED BY THOMAS MOORE

ROBERT FROST

The Rose Family

The rose is a rose,
And was always a rose.
But the theory now goes
That the apple's a rose,
And the pear is, and so's
The plum, I suppose.
The dear only knows
What will next prove a rose.
You, of course, are a rose—
But were always a rose.

JO SHAPCOTT

Rosa foetida

I'm an imperfect thing:
neat, layered
but spilling petals and pollen,
dropping bruised scent

on to the ground.
Essence of roses is not sweet,
but brown at the edges
like the air you breathe.

Rosa pimpinellifolia

O I'm leaning
against your forehead,
against your eyelid,
scenting your skin

with my own,
making you think
you can sleep
inside my face.

Rosa odorata

I can't turn a smell
into a single word;
you've no right
to ask. Warmth
coaxes rose fragrance
from the underside of petals.

The oils meet air:
rhodinol is old rose;
geraniol, like geranium;
nerol is my essence
of magnolia; eugenol,
a touch of cloves.

D. H. LAWRENCE

Gloire de Dijon

When she rises in the morning
I linger to watch her;
She spreads the bath-cloth underneath the window
And the sunbeams catch her
Glistening white on the shoulders,
While down her sides the mellow
Golden shadow glows as
She stoops to the sponge, and her swung breasts
Sway like full-blown yellow
Gloire de Dijon roses.

She drips herself with water, and her shoulders
Glisten as silver, they crumple up
Like wet and falling roses, and I listen
For the sluicing of their rain-dishevelled petals.
In the window full of sunlight
Concentrates her golden shadow
Fold on fold, until it glows as
Mellow as the glory roses.

MARY ('PERDITA') ROBINSON

Ode to the Snowdrop

THE Snow-drop, Winter's timid child,
   Awakes to life, bedew'd with tears,
And flings around its fragrance mild;
And where no rival flowerets bloom,
Amidst the bare and chilling gloom,
   A beauteous gem appears!

All weak and wan, with head inclin'd,
   Its parent-breast the drifted snow,
It trembles, while the ruthless wind
Bends its slim form; the tempest lowers,
Its em'rald eye drops crystal show'rs
   On its cold bed below.

Poor flow'r! On thee the sunny beam
   No touch of genial warmth bestows!
Except to thaw the icy stream
   Whose little current purls along,
And whelms thee as it flows.

The night-breeze tears thy silky dress,
   Which decked with silvery lustre shone;
The morn returns, not thee to bless.—
   The gaudy *Crocus* flaunts its pride,

And triumphs where *its rival*—died
Unsheltered and unknown!

No sunny beam shall gild thy grave,
    No bird of pity thee deplore:
There shall no verdant branches wave,
        For spring shall all her gems unfold,
        And revel 'midst her beds of gold,
    When thou art seen no more!

Where'er I find thee, gentle flower,
    Thou still art sweet, and dear to me!
For I have known the cheerless hour,
        Have seen the sun-beams cold and pale,
        Have felt the chilling, wintry gale,
    And wept, and shrunk like thee!

OLIVE CUSTANCE

Rainbows — *Forget-me-nots*

A song of forget-me-nots I sing!
　　Forget-me-nots are my favourite flowers,
　　Love, because they are like your eyes.
　　Blue as the wild, blue butterflies
They stare and dream through the singing hours,
　　Under the turquoise and silver skies,
Under the fickle eyes of spring.

They see the sky like a looking-glass
　　That waits for the beautiful face of day,
　　　For the face of the dawn is cold.
　　　Stare with eyes more yellow than gold
When the noon sun sends the clouds away.
　　　And at twilight time, with gaze as bold,
They watch the pomps of sunset pass.

And sleepless under the starlit skies
　　They listen and look with their petals wide,
　　　For though the moon be lost for hours,
　　　Hidden behind her high cloud towers,
　　A brown bird sings by the river-side.
　　　Forget-me-nots are my favourite flowers,
Love, because they are like your eyes.

FREDA DOWNIE

Aconites

Winter holds fast,
But a little warmth escapes like sand
Through the closed fingers.
The error is annual and certain,
Letting the pygmy flowers
Make their prompt appearance
Under creaking trees.
They stand with serious faces, green ruffed,
As prim as Tudor portraits.

In the west
The greys and gleam slide in the wind
And only the descended blackbird
Augments the intrepid yellow.

SEAMUS HEANEY

Sweetpea

'What did Thought do?'
                              'Stuck
a feather in the ground and thought
it would grow a hen.'
                              Rod
by rod we pegged the drill for sweetpea
with light brittle sticks,
twiggy and unlikely in fresh mould,
and stalk by stalk we snipped
the coming blooms.
                              And so when pain
had haircracked her old constant vestal stare
I reached for straws and thought:
seeing the sky through a mat of creepers,
like water in the webs of a green net,
opened a clearing where her heart sang
without caution or embarrassment, once or twice.

LOUISE GLÜCK

Hyacinth

1

Is that an attitude for a flower, to stand
like a club at the walk; poor slain boy,
is that a way to show
gratitude to the gods? White
with colored hearts, the tall flowers
sway around you, all the other boys,
in the cold spring, as the violets open.

2

There were no flowers in antiquity
but boys' bodies, pale, perfectly imagined.
So the gods sank to human shape with longing.
In the field, in the willow grove,
Apollo sent the courtiers away.

3

And from the blood of the wound
a flower sprang, lilylike, more brilliant
than the purples of Tyre.
Then the god wept: his vital grief
flooded the earth.

4

Beauty dies: that is the source
of creation. Outside the ring of trees
the courtiers could hear
the dove's call transmit
its uniform, its inborn sorrow—
They stood listening, among the rustling willows.
Was this the god's lament?
They listened carefully. And for a short time
all sound was sad.

5

There is no other immortality:
in the cold spring, the purple violets open.
And yet, the heart is black,
there is its violence frankly exposed.
Or is it not the heart at the center
but some other word?
And now someone is bending over them,
meaning to gather them—

6

They could not wait
in exile forever.
Through the glittering grove
the courtiers ran
calling the name
of their companion

over the bird's noise,
over the willows' aimless sadness.
Well into the night they wept,
their clear tears
altering no earthly color.

IVOR GURNEY

Early Winter

I love chrysanthemums and winter jasmine,
Clustering lichened walls a century old;
That in my western ways when days draw in,
Grow in the farm gardens in the first cold.
Strange foreigners should prove
So homely to my love.

For all the age that lies upon this land
Seems to call out for things native, things like
Britain knew, when the tongue talked soft, and
Not yet Rome from the far Gaul might strike.
Yet here Japan
Has flowered, as after plan.

ADRIAN HENRI

Country Song

'Lily of the Valley (Convalaria Majalis, fam. Lilliaceae). Grows wild in N. England. Commonly cultivated. Flowers in May. Berries red when ripe. Leaves particularly poisonous because three constituents depress the heart, like Foxglove.'

What are the constituents that depress the heart?
the scent of lilies in the darkgreen silences under trees
milkweed and ragwort and sunshine in hedges
small flowers picked amongst trees when it's raining

A year ago
You planted lilies in the valley of my mind
There were lilies at the bottom of my garden
And ferrys at the bottom of my street

Now
I sit here in sunlight with the smell of wild garlic
Trying to taperecord the sound of windflowers and celandines

Wondering
What are the three constituents that depress the heart
Without you here in the country?

EDNA ST VINCENT MILLAY

The Strawberry Shrub

Strawberry Shrub, old-fashioned, quaint as quinces,
Hard to find in a world where neon and noise
Have flattened the ends of the three more subtle senses;
And blare and magenta are all that a child enjoys.

More brown than red the bloom—it is a dense colour;
Colour of dried blood; colour of the key of F.
Tie it in your handkerchief, Dorcas, take it to school
To smell. But no, as I said, it is browner than red; it is duller
Than history, tinnier than algebra; and you are colour-deaf.

Purple, a little, the bloom, like musty chocolate;
Purpler than the purple avens of the wet fields;
But brown and red and hard and hiding its fragrance;
More like an herb it is: it is not exuberant.
You must bruise it a bit: it does not exude; it yields.

ANNE RIDLER

Columbine and Larkspur

Six doves or dancers
Crowd on a stem with feet for balance
Pointed askance:
Or cones of glass
Or cockle hats hung on a hidden thread.
If there were doves of yellow and red
If songs were buds
                    If birds had
The stillness of sap and flight were frozen . . .
Here on a stem
Move
   The dancers but will not leave.
If there were doves
This colour and dolphin-birds this blue . . .
The garden breaks
In a thousand stained-glass fragments. Who
Sees and makes
                    The ordered picture
With these above and these below
That these should fly and these should grow,
With leads to fix
Wings and calyx
And keeps the clue?

But now
      They bow
Set and exchange as dancers do.

D. H. LAWRENCE

Red Geranium and Godly Mignonette

Imagine that any mind ever *thought* a red geranium!
As if the redness of a red geranium could be anything but a
    sensual experience
and as if sensual experience could take place before there were
    any senses.
We know that even God could not imagine the redness of a red
    geranium
nor the smell of mignonette
when geraniums were not, and mignonette neither.
And even when they were, even God would have to have a nose
    to smell at the mignonette.
You can't imagine the Holy Ghost sniffing at cherry-pie
    heliotrope.
Or the Most High, during the coal age, cudgelling his mighty
    brains
even if he had any brains: straining his mighty mind
to think, among the moss and mud of lizards and mastodons
to think out, in the abstract, when all was twilit green and
    muddy:
'Now there shall be tum-tiddly-um, and tum-tiddly-um,
hey-presto! scarlet geranium!'
We know it couldn't be done.
But imagine, among the mud and the mastodons

god sighing and yearning with tremendous creative yearning, in
    that dark green mess
oh, for some other beauty, some other beauty
that blossomed at last, red geranium, and mignonette.

KATHLEEN RAINE

The Herm

Blind I know with senses arising from fern and tree,
Blind lips and fingers trace a god no eyes can see,
Blind I touch love's monster form that bounds
My world of field and forest, crowns my hills.
Blind I worship a blind god in his hour
Whose serpent-wand over my soul has power
To lead the crowding souls back from the borders of death,
Heaven's swift-winged fiat, earth's primeval monolith.

Notes

The Garden

R. S. Thomas, *The Garden* (p. 11)
R. S. Thomas (1913–2000) was ordained in 1937 and spent his life
in the service of the Church of England in a succession of Welsh
rural parishes until 1978 when he retired to Rhiw on the Llyn
peninsula in north Wales. In 1994 he returned to Anglesey where
he had spent part of his childhood. This tight-lipped sonnet turns
not on the eighth but the tenth line, 'It is the old kingdom of man,'
to explain in four verses the peculiar satisfaction of gardening. (See
also poem on p. 141.)

Nicholas Grimald, *The Garden* (p. 12)
Nicholas Grimald (1519–1562) was a scholar rather than a gardener;
throughout his career, as a student at Cambridge, then a fellow of
Merton College, Oxford, and even as Bishop Ridley's chaplain, he
would have been surrounded by gardens and encouraged to walk in
them for his better health. In this poem, published in Tottel's
Miscellany in 1557, he describes the usual kind of walled garden
attached to such establishments, with its beds of salad vegetables
and herbs shaded by pleached trees, and warm walls clad with
grapes, and beds of flowers that adorn the 'mould', that is, the earth.

Nicholas Breton, *A Strange Description of a rare Garden Plot* (p. 14)
Nicholas Breton (1545?–1626?), the 'Passionate Shepherd', presents
a knot garden as an emblem of his own mental state, walled by the
patience that keeps his chagrin bottled up, hedged with 'care', that
is, anxiety, while its irrigation channel flows with tears. The pattern

of the garden is quadripartite; to the motifs of love, showing entwined hearts, of yet more care, marked out with thyme which is a pun on time, and friendship, set with pennyroyal, is added a fourth set with bachelor's buttons, an old name for feverfew, and surrounded by 'maiden-hair', probably *Adiantum capillus-veneris*.

Andrew Marvell, *The Garden* (p. 16)
As a young graduate of Trinity College, Cambridge, Andrew Marvell (1621–1678) served as tutor to Mary Fairfax, daughter of the great Civil War general, at his house at Nun Appleton, in Yorkshire. His praise of the garden is a later exercise in the same tradition as Grimald's, and the garden too is similar. In Marvell's metaphysical imagination nothing is simple; though he celebrates greenery and solitude, he includes products of the latest sophistication of the gardener's art, nectarines and peaches which were trained on warm walls, and melons which were grown in stove-houses for the master's table. (See also poem on p. 145.)

John Clare, *The Cottage Garden* (p. 19)
This cluster of Spenserian stanzas, written by John Clare (1793–1864) describes the kind of garden he would have seen as a child around his parents' cottage in Helpston, Cambridgeshire, where he too took a cottage in the 1820s. Everything about it is familiar, from the black house bee (*Bombus lapidarius*) to the white moth in the elder (*Sambucus nigra*), the sparrow and the wormwood (*Artemisia absinthum*) and mallow (*Malva sylvestris*), both common weeds, growing by the door. The actual gardening is done by children transplanting wayside plants to the shelter of the cottage walls and the hedge of privet (*Ligustrum vulgare*).

Thomas Hardy, *Where They Lived* (p. 21)
This short lyric by Thomas Hardy (1840–1928) compresses a

wealth of complex feeling that is instantly familiar to anyone who has revisited the garden of his childhood and found it derelict. 'Bents' are the reedy grasses, that will take over when mowing is left off. (See also poems on pp. 67, 71 and 152.)

George Herbert, *Paradise – The Gardener's Prayer* (p. 22)
For George Herbert (1593–1633) verse composition was a private devotional exercise, in which he developed meditations on emblematic themes, disciplining his imagination by imposing pre-ordained patterning, in this case a particularly demanding sight-rhyme scheme. Herbert asks God to 'enclose' him so that he will not 'start', as if he were a plant to be blanched or shaded to stop it bolting, to be sharp to him to stop his growth becoming rank, and to prune and pare him. Herbert suffered all his life from ill-health; he had not completed his third year at Bemerton when he died of consumption.

John Scott of Amwell, *The Garden – Epistle to a Friend* (p. 23)
John Scott (1730–1783) was a London Quaker, born in Bermondsey; when he was ten his family moved to Amwell, in Hertfordshire. In 1776 he published *Amwell*, a descriptive poem, which was well received. This kind of Horatian 'Epistle to a Friend' was already old-fashioned and, of Scott's chosen arbiters of gardening taste, Capability Brown (1715–1783) and Horace Walpole (1717–1797), the landscape engraver, William Woollett (1735–1785) and the poet William Mason (1724–1797), were those of a previous generation, Scott's preference for an agricultural landscape being not Romantic but Virgilian.

Norman Nicholson, *A Garden Enclosed* (p. 27)
Norman Nicholson (1914–1997) lived all his life in the mining town of Millom in Cumbria, close to the famous ironmines of

Hodbarrow that went from boom in the sixties to bust in the eighties. His Latin title meaning 'enclosed garden' is an ironic reference to representations of Paradise in mediaeval iconography. Nicholson makes of his urban garden a safe place for the Christ-child who may be any child of the people. *Osmunda regalis* is commonly known as royal fern; the 'pale green butterfly', a female Brimstone (*Gonopteryx rhamni*), would have laid her eggs on a buckthorn.

Nathaniel Hookes, *To Amanda Walking in the Garden* (p. 29)
In 1653, his last year at Trinity College Cambridge, Nathaniel Hookes (1628–1712) published a book of poems celebrating an imaginary lady he called 'Amanda', the loving one. The convention of praising ladies walking in gardens is an ancient one, but few poets would go so far as to depict the plants becoming more erect, especially the 'short dwarf' tulip growing an inch, and other flowers popping up as by the 'scaffold method spring'. This elaboration of the pathetic fallacy justifies the poet begging Amanda to let him mark her gown with green by tumbling her in the grass.

Alfred, Lord Tennyson, *Amphion* (p. 31)
In classical mythology Amphion was given a lyre by Hermes; when he and his twin brother were charged with building the lower city at Thebes, Amphion was able to move his share of the stones into place by making them dance to his music. Tennyson seems to confuse Amphion with Orpheus, who could make trees dance. This poem is usually dated 1837–8, and was perhaps written when the Tennysons were living at High Beech in Epping Forest. A 'galopade' was a fashionable Hungarian-style dance of the 1830s; a 'poussette' is a kind of country dance. (See also poem on p. 78.)

Anna Wickham, A *House in Hampstead* (p. 35)
Anna Wickham (1884–1947) was born in Wimbledon, educated in
Australia, at Sydney Girls' High, and returned to England when she
was 21. She trained for the opera but married the astronomer
Patrick Hepburn, much mocked as 'Croydon Man', instead. In 1940
she wrote to a friend, 'I am keeping this house which adjoins
Hampstead Heath where it has been trenched against parachutists'.

The Gardener

Horace, Book I, *Satire VIII. Complaint of Priapus* (p. 39)
Horace's satire is spoken by an effigy of Priapus, the god of gardens.
Such an effigy with red painted face and huge projecting phallus
('something else as red as scarlet') was set in a garden to frighten
birds and other pests. In mythology Priapus was the son born to
Aphrodite as a result of her intercourse with Dionysus or possibly
Adonis. In this case the garden has been made out of an old burying
ground where witches come to sacrifice and cast spells. Philip
Francis (1708–1773), whose version this is, was considered the best
translator of Horace by Dr Johnson, himself no mean Horatian.

Ruth Pitter, *Aged Cupid* (p. 42)
Ruth Pitter (1897–1992) was born of artisan parents in Ilford and
went to school in Bow but her love of growing things was born of
the summer holidays that the family spent in a cottage in rural
Essex. Though she was a close friend and inspiration to C. S. Lewis
for many years, few studies of his life and career give any space to
his relationship with her. In all she published eighteen collections
of verse. 'Bat-willow' is *Salix alba*, out of which cricket bats are
made. (See also poems on pp. 57, 104, 112 and 159.)

Rowland Watkyns, *The Gardener* (p. 45)

In this poem from *Flamma sine fumo* (1662), Rowland Watkyns (1616?–1664) takes as his text John 20 which tells how Mary Magdalen came seeking where Jesus' body had been laid after being taken down from the cross, and found someone standing in the garden, whom she took to be the gardener. He was in fact the risen Christ. Watkyns argues that God who designed Eden is the only divine gardener, who knows how to get the best out of us. He then moves to the symbol of the womb of the Blessed Virgin as the enclosed garden that harboured the Saviour before His birth, as the garden would shelter Him after death.

George William Frederick Howard, Viscount Morpeth,
To a Jasmine-Tree (p. 46)

This poem, printed in *Heath's Book of Beauty* for 1834, was penned by the 32-year-old son and heir of the sixth Earl of Carlisle, then MP for the West Riding of Yorkshire. The 'jasmine-tree' was probably *Jasminum officinalum*. Nawarth or Naworth Castle, is the hereditary seat of the earls of Carlisle; the 'border tower' is nowadays referred to as the Dacre Tower. 'Belted Will' is Lord William Howard, third son of the fourth duke of Norfolk, who married Elizabeth Dacre, heiress to the disputed Dacre estates, including Naworth Castle which he restored. He was dubbed 'belted Will' by Sir Walter Scott who in *The Lay of the Last Minstrel* attributed to him the heroic exploits of his Dacre forebears.

Douglas Dunn, *Gardeners* (p. 48)

Douglas Dunn, Professor of English Language and Literature at St Andrews until 1999, was born in Inchinnan, Renfrewshire, in 1942. He had worked as a librarian under Philip Larkin in the University Library at Hull. He does most of his writing with a 2B pencil in a summer house in his garden. 1789 is of course the year of the French Revolution.

John Burnside, *The Solitary in Autumn* (p. 50)
John Burnside was born in Fife in 1955, and worked for some years as a software engineer before deciding to devote himself full-time to writing. He now makes his home in Surrey.

Freda Downie, *Her Garden* (p. 52)
Freda Downie (1929–1993), who lived most of her life in Hertfordshire, was one of the circle of Berkhamsted poets, with John Mole, John Cotton and Fred Sedgwick, but did not publish her work until the 1970s. Silvertown is the name given to the area between the city airport and the Thames, near the Thames Flood Barrier. The ships parked at the end of the road were anchored in the Royal Victoria and George V docks. Grandmother's 'tiger-' or 'cinnamon lilies' are probably garden hybrids bred from any of the species listed as having spicy scent, *Lilium auratum, L. duchartrei, L. papilliferum, L. sulphureum,* and *L. wallichianum.* (See also poems on pp. 151 and 191.)

David Constantine, *The Pitman's Garden* (p. 53)
David Constantine, translator of Hölderlin, Goethe, Michaux and Jacottet, was born in Salford in 1944; since 1981 he has been the Fellow in German at Queen's College, Oxford. This poem, dedicated to a member of the department of continuing education at Durham University and his wife, is set in Durham, where the ruined chapel of the mediaeval Hospital of Mary Magdalen is to be found on the north side of Gilesgate near the old railway station. (See also poem on p. 131.)

U. A. Fanthorpe, *Men on Allotments* (p. 55)
U. A. Fanthorpe, who was born in Kent, near Biggin Hill in 1929, and now lives in Wotton under Edge in Gloucestershire, began writing poetry in her forties. She says, 'I am aware in daily life that the people I meet are more perceptive, braver and more practical than I am — and out of perversity I like to celebrate this.' (See also poems on pp. 76 and 178.)

Ruth Pitter, *The Diehards* (p. 57)
When this poem was written, in 1941, 1,400,000 Britons were digging for victory. Parks, commons, meadows, lawns and flowerbeds had been dug up to provide homegrown food, so that all available shipping could be devoted to the war effort. (See also poems on pp. 42, 104, 112 and 159.)

Elizabeth Jennings, *Her Garden* (p. 59)
Elizabeth Jennings (1926–2002) lived all her life in Oxford, where she had ample opportunity to observe the gardening of others. She was a mystical poet who would well have understood the sacredness of the emblem of the 'hortus conclusus'. The superstition she refers to in the first lines, that flowers should not be picked at the full moon, is of a different, pagan order. The third quatrain seems to refer to menopause, when fecundity ends, but in Jennings's sensitive hands, decay holds no threat and causes no rancour. (See also poem on p. 133.)

Phoebe Hesketh, *Death of a Gardener* (p. 60)
Phoebe Hesketh was born in Preston in 1909 and since 1948 has published fifteen collections of verse. She has lived all her life in rural Lancashire from where she draws her poetic inspiration. (See also poem on p. 139.)

Ben Jonson, *To Thomas Palmer* (p. 61)
Thomas Palmer was a Catholic scholar who, when forced out of
Oxford in 1566, retired to his estate in Essex where he prepared two
books of botanical emblems, 'The Sprite of Trees and Herbs' and
'Two hundred Poosees'. For the 'carbuncle in Aaron's breast', see
Exodus xxviii:17 and xxxix:10. The 'seven-fold flower of art' is the
seven liberal arts. Ben Jonson (1572–1637) wrote these verses in
about 1599, to stand as a commendation at the head of one or other
of Palmer's works, neither of which was ever published.

The Seasons

William Shakespeare, *Spring versus Winter* (p. 65)
This song, a version of the old debate between Hiems (winter) and
Ver (spring) is performed at the end of *Love's Labour's Lost* (c.
1592). The 'daisies pied' are not spotted but 'pie-eyed'; 'lady-
smocks' are a common name for the mauve-white cuckoo flower,
Cardamine pratensis, which comes into bloom at the same time as
the first cuckoo is heard. All attempts to identify the yellow
'cuckoo-buds' are simply guesses. 'Roasted crabs' are crab apples
roasted in the fire until they swell then dunked in ale to make the
foamy sweet called 'lamb's wool'.

Thomas Hardy, *Weathers* (p. 67)
Hardy's version contrasts spring and winter. His 'chestnut spikes'
are the blossoms of the horse chestnut (*Aesculus hippocastanum*).
(See also poems on pp. 21, 71 and 152.)

Samuel Taylor Coleridge, *On Observing a Blossom on the First of
February 1796* (p. 68)
Coleridge (1772–1834) does not identify the blossom he catches
sight of, apparently during a mild spell. 'Blue voluptuous eye' is a

quotation from the second part of Erasmus Darwin's *The Botanic Garden* published in 1792 (II. ii. 307); 'Bristowa's bard' is the poet Thomas Chatterton of Bristol, who died by his own hand at the age of 17; 'Poland's hope' was Tadeusz Kosciusko, defeated in battle in 1795, but not in fact dead as Coleridge thought.

Philip Larkin, *Coming* (p. 70)
This poem was completed on 25 February 1950. Larkin, who died in 1985, was 28. (See also poems on pp. 97 and 135.)

Thomas Hardy, *A Backward Spring* (p. 71)
Generally Hardy's observation of nature is accurate. In this cold spring the snowdrops (*Galanthus nivalis*), which have a long blooming period, are still out, and the primroses (*Primula vulgaris*) are coming into bloom but the barberry (*Berberis* spp.) hangs fire. The evergreen myrtle (*Myrtis communis*), being only half-hardy in the British Isles and having been already burnt by frost in mid-December, might not bloom at all or indeed ever again. (See also poems on pp. 21, 67 and 152.)

Anon [Sir Thomas Browne?] *Early Spring* (p. 72)
These seven lines are to be found in a commonplace book of Elizabeth Lyttelton, daughter of Sir Thomas Browne, the physician-littérateur of Norwich (1605–1682). Flowering almond trees don't grow wild in England in the company of birches and *Daphne mezereum*, the flowers of which come before the leaves. No British plant was ever known as mandrake though the dried root of White Bryony was certainly sold as a substitute for mandrake root. Crocuses, hyacinths, anemones, daffodils and hazels are all native to the British Isles, as is no plant of the genus Paronychia.

Richard Wilbur, *April 5, 1974* (p. 73)
Richard Wilbur was born in New York in 1921, of an artist father
and a journalist mother. In 1923 the family moved to a pre-
revolutionary house on a 400-acre estate at North Caldwell, New
Jersey. Wilbur was married in 1942, brought up four children in
western Massachusetts, and was appointed US Poet Laureate in
1987.

Muriel Spark, *Complaint in a Wash-out Season* (p. 74)
Despite her resounding success as a novelist, Dame Muriel Spark,
born 1918, has always thought of herself primarily as a poet. On her
return to Britain from South Africa in 1944, she took the position
of general secretary to the Poetry Society and editor of *The Poetry
Review*. Since 1968 she has lived in Tuscany.

e. e. cummings, *'i thank You God . . .'* (p. 75)
e. e. cummings (1894–1962) spent his vacations on the family
property, Joy Farm, near Madison, New Hampshire.

U. A. Fanthorpe, *May 8th: how to recognise it* (p. 76)
Fanthorpe gave up teaching at a prestigious girls' school to work as
a clerical assistant in a hospital, and what she witnessed there
provided the mainspring of her poetical inspiration. Her poems
about gardening are infrequent but invariably insightful. (See also
poems on pp. 55 and 178.)

Alfred, Lord Tennyson, *Summer Night* (p. 78)
This poem, an approximation of the stanzaic form of a *ghazal*, is
read aloud by Ida, feminist heroine of Tennyson's *The Princess*, after
she has been kissed by the Prince and 'Her falser self slipt from her
like a robe, And left her woman . . .'. She has been watching the
boy asleep and the poem she reads aloud is a direct sexual

invitation. Danaë, imprisoned in a tower by her anxious father, was visited (and impregnated) by Jupiter in the form of a shower of gold. (See also poem on p. 31.)

Hart Crane, *In Shadow* (p. 79)
Hart Crane (1899–1932) is generally considered a poet of the city. When his mother was divorced from his father he went to stay with her in Cuba on her father's plantation at the Isle of Pines. In this early poem, published in December 1917, when Crane was only eighteen, before he had emerged as an overt and aggressive homosexual and begun to destroy his life through alcohol addiction, he celebrates an equivocal relationship.

Fredegond Shove, *Twilight in November* (p. 80)
Fredegond Shove (1899–1949) is best known as the author of four lyrics set by Ralph Vaughan Williams. She was the daughter of F. W. Maitland, the biographer of Lesley Stephen, and Florence Fisher, a cousin of Virginia Woolf. In 1915 she married the Cambridge economist Gerald Shove, and made her home thereafter in Cambridge. In 1922 the Hogarth Press published a collection of her poems called *Daybreak*, from which this poem is taken.

Jenny Joseph, *The unlooked-for season* (p. 81)
Jenny Joseph, author of the nation's best loved poem, 'Warning' (When I am an old woman I shall wear purple . . .) was born in 1932 in Birmingham and now lives in Minchinhampton, Gloucestershire. Her latest publication is *Led by the Nose*, in which she describes a year in her garden through smells. She wrote this poem of late love in 1960, when she was but 28; she married the next year. Her husband died in 1985.

Stewart Conn, *Visiting Hour* (p. 82)
Stewart Conn was born in Glasgow in 1936 and worked for thirty
years as a producer of radio drama. This terse poem supplies the title
for the collection he published in 1978.

Anne Ridler, *Winter Poem* (p. 83)
For many years Anne Ridler (1912–2001) worked as an editor at
Faber and Faber; her husband was printer to the University of
Oxford. *Pyrus japonica* was the name given by the trade for more
than a century to the many garden varieties of *Chaenomeles speciosa*,
the Japanese quince, which often flowers at or even before
Christmas. 'Awns' are bristles projecting from a plant organ; Ridler
refers to the development of the long feathery styles on the seeds of
Clematis species. (See also poems on pp. 165, 180 and 199.)

The Gardener's Work

Matthew Arnold, *Quiet Work* (p. 87)
Arnold (1822–1888) had a terrible time with this sonnet, rewriting
it again and again, even after it was first published in 1849, and it is
still bedevilled by a deep confusion between the one lesson and the
two duties. Nevertheless the core idea, of unstressed, unbossed, self-
regulating labour, is a fundamental element in our enthusiasm for
gardening.

Fleur Adcock, *Under the Lawn* (p. 88)
Fleur Adock was born in Papakura, New Zealand in 1934; at the
outbreak of war her peace-worker parents came to England where
they remained until she was thirteen, when the family returned to
New Zealand. In 1963 Adcock, by then twice divorced, returned
to England with the younger of her two sons and worked as a
librarian for sixteen years. Her first collection of poems was

published in 1967. She has lived in East Finchley since 1971. (See also poem on p. 124.)

Robert Frost, *Putting in the Seed* (p. 89)
Robert Frost (1874–1963) grew up in Salem, New Hampshire. In 1900 he bought a property in Derry, New Hampshire and tried to combine poultry farming and teaching. In 1911 he and his wife came to England where this sonnet was written in 1914. Commentators concentrate on the clear sexual subtext of this poem; as interesting to a gardener is Frost's understanding of how we watch for signs of germination and how they appear. (See also poems on pp. 94, 98, 176 and 184.)

Edward Thomas, *Sowing* (p. 90)
Tall, shy, melancholy Edward Thomas (1878–1917) wrote no poetry until December 1914, when he was living in the Gloucestershire village of Dymock. It was Robert Frost, who was also living in the village at the time, who encouraged him to write. This poem was written at Yew-Tree Cottage, Steep, near Petersfield on 23 March 1915, a day after the vernal equinox, not long before Thomas enlisted.

Duncan Bush, *The Hook* (p. 91)
Duncan Bush, born in Cardiff in 1946, graduated from Warwick University in 1978, and went on to Wadham College, Oxford. He now lives in rural Powys. He says, 'Writing is like farming. You have a certain area of land, of a certain soil type, and all you can hope is to work in it all your life.' The tool Bush is celebrating seems to be some kind of bill-hook; the continental sickle is not ambidextrous and does not cut both ways.

Robert Frost, *The Objection to Being Stepped on* (p. 94)
Frost is well aware that the son of Cain beat weapons into

ploughshares; his joke is that he reverses the process. It seems that the poet-gardener was bending and proceeding backwards when he trod on the hoe which whacked him on the behind. (See also poems on pp. 89, 98, 176 and 184.)

Seamus Heaney, *The Pitchfork* (p. 95)
Seamus Heaney, born in 1939, spent the first twelve years of his life on the family farm near Mossbawn, 35 miles north-west of Belfast. The pitchfork he writes about is of the kind that were used to build haystacks, that must pick up the hay cleanly and toss it accurately on to the summit of the stack. (See also poems on pp. 101 and 192.)

William Empson, *Rolling the Lawn* (p. 96)
William Empson (1906–1984) lived much of his life outside England, as an academic in Tokyo, Beijing and America; he was in England during the war and from 1952 he was professor at Sheffield University. 'Our final hope is flat despair' is from Belial's speech in Book II of *Paradise Lost*. The garden roller he sees as a fetish, distinguishing it from the 'Texas Pope', by which he means the leader of the Holy Roller cult. 'Roll not the abdominal wall' refers to an advertisement for an exercise gadget, a weighted mini-roller held with both hands and worked backwards and forwards by someone kneeling on the floor.

Philip Larkin, *Cut Grass* (p. 97)
Larkin completed this little masterpiece on 3 June 1971. It is a meditation on Isaiah xl:6 'All flesh is grass and all the goodliness thereof is as the flower of the field'. 'Chestnut flowers' are horse-chestnut flowers (*Aesculus hippocastanum*); the hedges are hawthorn (*Crataegus monogyna*). 'Queen Anne's lace' is more often called cow-parsley (*Anthriscus sylvestris*). (See also poems on pp. 70 and 135.)

Robert Frost, *Gathering Leaves* (p. 98)
Unlike Larkin, who never got his hands into the soil, Frost has done all the jobs in the garden. Anyone who has collected leaves for making mulch knows that a shedful of leaves will degrade to a bucketful but the nutrients mulched leaves add to the soil are too valuable to waste in anything as easy as a bonfire. (See also poems on pp. 89, 94, 176 and 184.)

Edward Thomas, *Digging* (p. 100)
Few have been the poets who have written on the sheer pleasure of digging. In this poem, written in March–April 1915, Thomas locates it in smell. In December 1909 he had written to his friend Gordon Bottomley: 'For two months nearly I have been better, chiefly because I have had to work hard and regularly in the new garden clay . . . it had to be done & I kept at it day by day & it did me good almost against my will.' The wild carrot is *Daucus carota*; goutweed, *Aegopodium podagraria*.

Seamus Heaney, *Digging* (p. 101)
This, the first poem in Heaney's first full-length collection, published in 1966, is Heaney's mission statement. It is also a tribute to the skills of his father, imagined digging his garden in retirement, after long years of digging potatoes that his children gathered and bagged up for him, and slicing out fuel-peat in the bogland. (See also poems on pp. 95 and 192.)

Maxine Kumin, *Turning the Garden in Middle Age* (p. 103)
Maxine Kumin, born in Philadelphia in 1925, has raised three children, horses, dogs, cattle, sheep, and organic vegetables on two hundred acres in the Min Hills, near Warner, New Hampshire. Parsnips left in the ground grow hairy; 'puddingstone' is the name given to any composite rock formed of pebbles cemented

together; 'fool's gold' is iron pyrites, sometimes found in such conglomerates. The word 'marrow' suggests that the parsnip root has rotted.

Ruth Pitter, *The Morals of Pruning* (p. 104)
(See also poems on pp. 42, 57, 112 and 159.)

Theodore Roethke, *Cuttings, Cuttings – (later)* (p. 105)
Theodore Roethke (1908–1963) spent much of his childhood in the greenhouse run by his father and uncle in Saginaw, Michigan. His father died when Roethke was nineteen and in the same year his uncle committed suicide. Later, Roethke was to suffer recurring episodes of mental illness. The famous 'greenhouse lyrics' that open his 1948 collection, *The Lost Son*, are always treated as encoded psychological autobiography. What would fascinate a gardener, as distinct from an academic, is that Roethke so clearly apprehends the wonder and excitement of plant propagation and nurture, and finds objective, rather than subjective, correlatives for it. (See also poems on pp. 111 and 163.)

Carol Rumens, *Weeds* (p. 107)
Carol Rumens, born in Lewisham in 1944, now lives in Bangor, North Wales.

Walter De la Mare, *A Widow's Weeds* (p. 108)
Walter De la Mare (1873–1956) takes the idea of the weeds, dreary black draperies widows were once required to wear, and flips it over into the idea of gardening with weeds. The widow's garden has some plants that gardeners still extirpate, such as willow-herb (*Epilobium* spp.), toadflax (*Linaria* spp.), rough hawksbit, more often hawkbit (*Leontodon hispidus*), meadowsweet (*Filipendula ulmaria*), campion (*Silene* spp.), and clover (*Trifolium* spp.), but the others,

comfrey (*Symphytum* spp.), bugloss (*Echium vulgare*), teasel (*Dipsacus fullonum*), tansy (*Tanacetum vulgare*), brown bee orchis, more often orchid (*Ophrys fusca*), burnet (*Sanguisorba* spp.), thyme (*Thymus* spp.) are nowadays considered desirable.

P. J. Kavanagh, *Elder* (p. 109)

P. J. Kavanagh, born in Worthing in 1931, celebrates one of the greatest nuisances in any garden, *Sambucus nigra*. The tradition that Judas hanged himself from an elder dates from mediaeval times; Sir John Mandeville claimed to have seen the actual tree fast by the pool of Siloam; Christ's cross too was thought to have been made of elder. Country folk would remove any twig of elder that found its way into kindling for household fires.

D. H. Lawrence, *Leaves of Grass, Flowers of Grass* (p. 110)

D. H. Lawrence here takes on Walt Whitman, fastening onto his covert propaganda for his own preference for sex of a non-reproductive kind, and laying into it hammer and tongs. Of course grass has flowers. The family of grasses is called Gramineae, rather than graminiferae, but Lawrence needs the idea of 'seed-bearing' to make his point that maleness involves hyperfertility. Why he should think that Gramineae are related to the Liliaceae, I don't know. (See also poems on pp. 187 and 201.)

Theodore Roethke, '*Long Live the Weeds*' (p. 111)

Roethke's epigraph is from the last stanza of 'Inversnaid', by Gerard Manley Hopkins.

> What would the world be, once bereft
> Of wet and of wildness? Let them be left,
> O let them be left, wildness and wet;
> Long live the weeds and the wilderness yet.

(See also poems on pp. 105 and 163.)

Ruth Pitter, *The Tall Fruit-Trees* (p. 112)

Pitter's anxieties about the ethics of pruning (see above, Poem on p. 104) triumph in this poem, where plum, pear and apple tree have grown too high to reach, and keep their fruit for the birds. In later life Pitter was wont to say 'My ultimate aim is a cottage in some peaceful place and enough strength left for gardening, my great love. I should not mind poverty in the country.' (See also poems on pp. 42, 57 and 104.)

James Fenton, *The Fruit-Grower in War-time (and some of his enemies)* (p. 114)

James Fenton was born in 1949 in Lincoln. From 1973–5 he was in Indo-China, as a war-reporter. From 1994–9 he was Professor of Poetry at Oxford. His first-hand experience of horticulture has been gained on his property outside Oxford; he was fascinated by the way that scientific language 'used familiar words in an unfamilar way'. The apple blossom weevil is *Anthomos pomorum*, the leaf weevil, *Phyllobius* spp., the codling moth, *Cydia pomonella*, the sawfly, *Hoplocampa testudinea*, the capsid bugs, *Plesiocoris rugicollis*, the apple sucker, *Psylla mali*, the woolly aphid, *Eriosoma lanigerum*, and the winter moth, *Operophtera brumata*.

The Gardener's Companions

Charlotte Smith, *To a green-chafer, on a white rose* (p. 121)

In 1765 Charlotte Smith (1749–1806) was married off to a rich wastrel, to whom she was to bear ten children. This poem comes from *Conversations Introducing Poetry, chiefly on Subjects of Natural History for the Use of Children and Young Persons* published in 1804, by which time Smith was separated from her husband, living on her family estate at Bignor Park in Sussex and making her living as a professional writer. Her American editor identifies the green chafer as *Scarabeus nobilis*; in fact it is *Cetonia aurata*, a serious pest of roses. When they hatch from eggs laid in the soil, the chafer larvae feed on roots, corms and tubers, while the adult insect feeds on buds, leaves and flowers.

Anna Laetitia Barbauld, *The Caterpillar* (p. 122)
Anna Laetitia Barbauld (1745–1825) was born in Lincolnshire, grew up at Warrington, moved with her husband to Palgrave in Suffolk where she and her husband ran a boarding school for boys. After a trip to the continent she and her husband settled in Hampstead in 1786, and moved to Stoke Newington. The identity of her silver, blue and orange caterpillar remains a mystery.

Fleur Adcock, *An Emblem* (p. 124)
Though garden slugs (*Arion hortensis*) are hermaphrodite they do copulate in August–September, both heads to both tails, forming the sort of yin-yang ring that Adcock describes.
(See also poem on p. 88.)

Thom Gunn, *Considering the Snail* (p. 126)
Thom Gunn was born in Gravesend, Kent, in 1929 and educated at Trinity College, Cambridge. After forty years teaching at Berkeley he now lives in Cole Valley near San Francisco. For Gunn, who has always been forthright about his own homosexuality, it is important that the snail is hermaphrodite and actively, tirelessly, seeks a mate of its own kind.

Emily Dickinson, *Our little Kinsmen – after Rain* (p. 127)
Emily Dickinson (1831–1886) is perhaps the greatest of garden poets. As she spent her whole life in her parents' house in Amherst and seldom travelled outside it, the garden was her whole world. In this poem written in about 1864, 'Our little Kinsmen' are

earthworms, also known as angle worms (because they are used by anglers). The bird is most likely a robin. (See also poems on pp. 132 and 138.)

Vicki Feaver, *Glow Worm* (p. 128)
Vicki Feaver, born in Nottingham in 1943, is keenly aware of the sexiness of the garden. It seems likely that Feaver has been involved in the British glow-worm survey, set up in 1994 and on-going, which seeks to raise awareness of glow-worms in the hope of stemming the decline in the numbers of *Lampyris noctiluca* in Britain. The adult wingless female does not feed; 'the diet of liquefied snails' is eaten by the glow-worm larvae that inject small snails with a paralysing compound.

Richard Flecknoe, *The Ant* (p. 129)
No creature in the garden has been more often addressed by poets than the ant, possibly because of Æsop's fable of the ant and the grasshopper, but also because of the biblical injunction to the sluggard, to go to the ant, 'consider her ways and be wise' (Proverbs, vi:6). Richard Flecknoe, an Irish hack writer who is also supposed to have been a Catholic priest (d. 1678?), turns the conventional moral on its head, representing the busy ant as deluded about the importance of its petty concerns.

William Empson, *The Ants* (p. 130)
Empson's own note to this sonnet explains, 'The ants build mud galleries into trees to protect the greenfly they get sugar from and keep them warm in the nest during winter'. The image that fascinates him is of underground extruded into overground, with its human analogues of the Tube train. Ants herd aphids so that they can feed off the honey-dew, mostly partially digested sap, that they excrete. In return the ants fend off rapacious ladybird larvae and

other predators, and keep the aphid eggs safe over winter in the shelter of their nests.

David Constantine, *The Wasps* (p. 131)
This puzzling poem, which opens with a perfect evocation of the end of the apple season, seems based on a misunderstanding. The wasps massing on the glass would have been trying to get back to the nest, now cut off from them by the closed window. (See also poem on p. 53.)

Emily Dickinson, *Like Trains of Cars on Tracks of Plush* (p. 132)
The poem, written around 1872, opens with an evocation of the sound of the bumble bee, like a railroad car running on rails of plush; Dickinson then moves to the bees' apparently heavy structure. 'Ajar' sounds like their diagonal progress, and looks like their half-open wing span and perhaps their way of attacking narrow flowers from the side, 'velvet masonry' refers to their bulk, suspended on such small wings. (See also poems on pp. 127 and 138.)

Elizabeth Jennings, *The Ladybird's Story* (p. 133)
Jennings takes the point of view of a ladybird, *Coccinella* spp., travelling about on a human palm, secure from ill-treatment by the superstitious belief that a ladybird in the hand means money. The ladybird is called that after Our Lady, apparently because horticulturalists, aware of the valuable service performed by ladybird larvae in the control of greenfly, blessed the genus with that name. (See also poem on p. 59.)

Paul Muldoon, *Hedgehog* (p. 134)
Paul Muldoon, born in 1951, was for many years a radio producer in Northern Ireland before becoming an academic, and now lectures at Princeton.

Philip Larkin, *The Mower* (p. 135)

It is no easy matter to imagine the Hull University librarian sitting on a ride-on mower, but every gardener is aware of the sick regret that follows the accidental killing of a garden creature. When this poem was written, in 1979, Larkin had only six years to live. He seems to have recognised, in this sudden spasm of sharp regret, that his own capacity for love was unused. (See also poems on pp. 70 and 97.)

Sylvia Plath, *Blue Moles* (p. 136)

Sylvia Plath (1932–63) was a perfectionist in everything including baking, bee-keeping and gardening. Gardens were central to her thinking. In 'A Comparison' (1961) she imagined the novelist engaged in 'pruning a rosebush with a large pair of shears' but poems were harder: 'I'm talking about the smallish, unofficial garden variety poem. How shall I describe it?— a door opens, a door shuts. In between you have had a glimpse, a garden, a person, a rainstorm, a dragonfly, a heart, a city.'

Emily Dickinson, *Within my Garden, rides a Bird* (p. 138)

The nearest English analogue to the tiny humming-bird in this poem of about 1862 would be the hawk-moth that can be sensed rather than seen as it whirrs around English gardens at dusk. Dickinson's neighbour Gregor Jenkins wrote of her after her death, 'Her garden was her source of constant joy, and on it she lavished the most affectionate care and attention . . . she sometimes stood on an old red army blanket when the ground was damp and frequently kneeled to reach her flowers.' (See also poems on pp. 127 and 132.)

Phoebe Hesketh, *Blue Tits* (p. 139)

The blue tit, *Parus caeruleus*, feeds, as Hesketh observes, on insects and larvae, often by streamsides and in reed-beds, throughout the year. In spring, when they are breeding, the much smaller tits will mob a single sparrow if it strays into their nesting territory, but when much larger rooks and crows carry off their nestlings they can only utter their 'cherr err err' protest from the sidelines. These days it is the sparrow which is becoming rare. (See also poem on p. 60.)

Anonymous, *The Blackbird* (p. 140)
The species that contributes most generously to the birdsong to be heard in British gardens is not the nightingale (*Luscinia megarynchos*) but the blackbird (*Turdus merula*) which is usually resident and largely ubiquitous. Its song is as inventive as the nightingale's, but more melodious and less percussive. As it often sings by night, especially where there is street lighting, it is often mistaken for the nightingale. This song was published in *Songs and Psalms* by J. Mundy in 1594.

R. S. Thomas, *Swifts* (p. 141)
The only amusement Thomas regularly permitted himself was bird-watching. The swift regularly seen in northern Europe is *Apus apus*. Thomas describes their habit of flying in formation at great speed, wheeling over the rooftops and uttering a looping thread of high-pitched screaming. (See also poem on p. 11.)

Grace Tollemache, *The Swallow's Note* (p. 142)
Though the Honourable Grace Emma Tollemache published four collections of verse between 1901 and 1916, she appears in no bibliographies of the period. The gardens of her childhood were those of Helmingham Hall, near Stowmarket in Suffolk, the seat of Lord Tollemache, now open to the public. When the swallow's plaintive 'vit-vit' becomes audible, summer has passed its peak.

The Gardener's Machinations

Andrew Marvell, *The Mower against Gardens* (p. 145)

The mower, who works in open fields, inveighs against the creation of discrete environments for prize plants, the breeding of hybrid pinks, roses, tulips, and grafting of fruit trees. The Marvel of Peru, *Mirabilis jalapa*, is commonly known as 'Four-o'clocks'. We can only imagine how Marvell's mower would react if he encountered geneticists exultant over developing a blue rose, or making lilies that glow in the dark by introducing genes from beetles or jelly-fish. (See also poem on p. 16.)

Simon Armitage, *Greenhouse* (p. 147)

Simon Armitage, born in 1963, was working as a probation officer in Manchester in 1989 when he wrote this poem about the greenhouse he helped his father to build out of the old (and now illegal) sash windows of the house they lived in. Besides being a very good example of the shock of the familiar that characterises his work, it is a moving tribute to the memory of his father.

William Cowper, *The Pine-Apple and the Bee* (p. 149)

All his life William Cowper (1731–1800) was plagued by cyclothymic disorder. During his slow recovery from a long period of delusional mania in the mid 1770s, he took up gardening. In 1779 he wrote to his cousin Joseph Hill, about the arrival of the Jamaica fleet, 'I hope it imports some pine-apple plants for me'. Pineapples, so-called because of their resemblance to pine-cones, were introduced to England from South America in the mid-seventeenth century to be grown in stove-houses.

Freda Downie, *Ferns* (p. 151)

Ferneries were an essential adjunct of the Victorian conservatory. Downie's modest version is a lean-to, with whitewashed shelving and glazed roof. 'Yadwigha' comes from the caption written by the Douanier Rousseau for his painting Le Rêve (1910) which shows a nude girl propped on a sofa amid fantastic plants in a moonlit jungle: 'Yadwigha dans un beau rêve s'étant endormie doucement entendait les sons d'une musette . . .' He later explained that Yadwigha was a Polish girl he had known in his youth. (See also poems on pp. 52 and 191.)

Thomas Hardy, *The Frozen Greenhouse – (St Juliot)* (p. 152)
From 1885 Hardy made his home at Max Gate, south-west of Dorchester. (See also poems on pp. 21, 67 and 71.)

Robert Graves, *The Florist Rose* (p. 154)
In this poem, first published in 1938, Robert Graves (1895–1985) develops Marvell's point, celebrating the florist's long stemmed single rose as a marvel of technology as unlike a living flower as an aeroplane is a bird. More importantly perhaps for Graves this perfect bloom cannot perform the mythologic function of the generic rose; it represents a discontinuity with tradition.

Amy Clampitt, *High Culture* (p. 155)
Amy Clampitt (1920–1994) was born in New Providence, Iowa, and lived most of her life in New York. It was not until 1974 that any of her poetry was published, and her first full-length book of poems did not appear until 1983. Her 'amaryllis' would now be called Hippeastrum; the bulbs were introduced into Europe from the Andes in the 1820s, and subsequently hybridised for forcing indoors in winter. The amaryllis is the subject of poems also by James Lasdun and Jorie Graham.

Louis MacNeice, *Flower Show* (p. 157)
Louis MacNeice (1907–1963) depicts a man who is trapped in the

marquee of a flower-show and, unable to escape from the dazzling glare of the massed giant blooms, succumbs to an epileptic fit.

Medbh McGuckian, *Gentians* (p. 158)
An alpine house is a greenhouse designed to replicate the climatic conditions that prevail at high altitudes, a dry, cold winter (as if under a blanket of snow), followed by a bright but wet spring, and a cool dry summer and autumn. McGuckian's gentians might be any of the 100 species known to grow in Tibet. Her description of their cultivation has more to do with human obstetrics than is immediately apparent. 'Husbands' knots' is the name given to extra-tight suturing of the perineum after childbirth. The 'dewfall of summer limes', actually the excreta of aphids, cannot reach the treasured alpine plants which are separated from them by glass and kept spotlessly clean, ventilated and dry to avoid the ever-present threat of botrytis.

Ruth Pitter, *Pot-bound* (p. 159)
Pitter's 'Pot-bound' would be just the usual moralisation of the gardening process if it were not for the fact that she describes pot-boundness and the ways of dealing with it so accurately that her words could be used as a mnemonic for students at horticultural college. (See also poems on pp. 42, 57, 104 and 112.)

Alice Oswald, *The Melon Grower* (p. 161)
Alice Oswald was trained as a classicist but now works as a gardener at Dartington Hall in Devon.

Theodore Roethke, *Transplanting* (p. 163)
Roethke said of the greenhouse that it was 'both heaven and hell . . . it was a universe, several worlds which, even as a child, one worried about and struggled to keep alive'. (See also poems on pp. 105 and 111.)

Kathleen Raine, *The Trees in Tubs* (p. 164)
Kathleen Raine (1908–) studied botany and zoology at Girton College, Cambridge; she later became a specialist in William Blake and the neo-Platonic tradition in English literature. According to Apollodorus and Plutarch, the laurel or bay tree, *Laurus nobilis*, came into existence when the mountain nymph Daphne, pursued by Apollo, called upon the gods for assistance and was metamorphosed into an evergreen tree. Apollo as god of poetry is crowned with bays, and we still call the national poet, the poet laureate. Like many of the Lauraceae, the laurel is dioecious; the male trees therefore do not bear fruit, reinforcing the notion that the tree is virginal. (See also poem on p. 203.)

Anne Ridler, *Azalea in the House* (p. 165)
What most people call azaleas are actually members of the genus Rhododendron, differing from the others in that they bear their flowers singly rather than in trusses. Azaleas bred for pot culture can be forced to bloom by removing them from an environment kept cold and dry and replicating the conditions of an alpine spring. The prophet is Elijah, who 'was as a fire and his words burnt like a torch' (Ecclesiasticus xlviii:1). The azalea is bright red, like the seraphim in duecento painting.
(See also poems on pp. 83, 180 and 199.)

William Cowper, *Inscription for a Moss-house in the Shrubbery at Weston* (p. 166)
Shrubberies, orchestrated plantings of shrubs and bushes, first made their appearance in English gardens in the eighteenth century; Cowper is one of the first English writers to use the term, as in 'The Shrubbery. Written in a Time of Affliction'. A moss-house was an arbour-like shelter lined and covered with carefully cut and fitted

moss. This poem of Cowper's, published in 1793, is the first mention of a moss-house in English. Cowper had moved to the village of Weston in 1786.

The Gardener's Reward

Ivor Gurney, *The Garden* (p. 169)
Ivor Gurney (1890–1937) was born in Gloucester, and loved the local countryside. His obvious talent secured him first a place at the King's School in Gloucester and then at the Royal College of Music. He was wounded and gassed in 1917; after spells at various military hospitals, he had a major breakdown, and was diagnosed as suffering from 'deferred shellshock'. His mental condition deteriorated and in 1922 he was committed to an asylum. Much of his poetry was written while he was institutionalised. The rose is 'ink-proud' because she has been celebrated by more poets than any other flower.

Katherine Pierpoint, *The Dreaming Bean* (p. 170)
Katherine Pierpoint was born in Northamptonshire in 1961 and studied languages at Exeter University. After working as a goatherd in France and touring Italy with a Bavarian brass band, she now lives in West London.

Charles Tomlinson, *Parsnips* (p. 172)
For 36 years Charles Tomlinson, born in Stoke-on-Trent in 1927, taught literature at the University of Bristol. Though he lives in Gloucestershire, he is probably better known as a poet in the USA, where he made his mark as the editor and friend of William Carlos Williams. Ted Chamberlin to whom this poem is dedicated is Professor of English and Comparative Literature at the University of Toronto, and a well-known supporter of hunter-gatherer peoples

in their attempts to prove their claims to their traditional lands on the evidence of their oral traditions.

Edward Thomas, *Swedes* (p. 173)
Before deep-freezes became common, swedes and other root vegetables were overwintered in a corner of the garden in a clamp, that is to say, they were carefully bedded in dry straw which was roofed over with earth. Thomas's poem, written in January 1915, celebrates the opening of the clamp and the discovery of the vegetables preserved within.

Alexander Pope, *The Gardens of Alcinous* (p. 174)
Though Pope (1688–1744) was a gardener, and made himself a garden at Twickenham, he wrote very little verse about gardening. This translation from the seventh book of the Odyssey was included in an essay on gardens that Pope wrote for the *Guardian*, No. 173, September 1713. Scheria, the realm of Alcinous, grandson of Poseidon, king of the Phaeacians, is understood to be modern-day Corfu.

Robert Frost, *After Apple-picking* (p. 176)
In this poem Frost subtly parallels his own stage of life to the season, turning the contradictions between the completion of the apples' fruiting cycle and the careful storing of the fruit, and his own condition of helplessness before his human destiny. Of his own 'fruit', his first son died in infancy, one daughter committed suicide and another was declared insane and institutionalised in 1947. (See also poems on pp. 89, 94, 98 and 184.)

U. A. Fanthorpe, *Pomona and Vertumnus* (p. 178)
Pomona is the Roman goddess of fruit-bearing trees. Vertumnus is the god of changing seasons, and especially of autumn. In

Metamorphoses 14 Ovid tells how Vertumnus assumed various shapes to court Pomona who had shut herself up in her orchard safe from the approach of men. In Fanthorpe's poem he succeeds in his suit as an old woman; in Ovid he reverts to his own shape so that Vertumnus and Pomona are a conventional heterosexual couple. Silvanus is a generic name for a haunter of the woods. Picus was a handsome boar-hunter transformed into a woodpecker by Circe whose advances he rejected (*Metamorphoses* 14) hence 'yaffle-headed', 'yaffle' being another name for the green woodpecker. Bramley is a variety of cooking-apple. (See also poems on pp. 55 and 76.)

Anne Ridler, *Picking Pears* (p. 180)
(See also poems on pp. 83, 165 and 199.)

Anacreontea 55, *The Rose* (p. 181)
The Anacreontea are poems written at a much later date in imitation or celebration of the poet Anacreon, a Greek lyric poet of the mid-sixth century BC famous for his praises of wine, women and song, only fragments of which have survived. This translation by the Irish poet Thomas Moore (1779–1852), published in 1800, was much admired by Byron. Dione is the goddess of the oak-tree on whom Jupiter fathered Venus. Cytherea is another name for Venus who rose out of the sea somewhere near the island of Cythera. 'Our rosy fillets' are the chaplets of roses with which banqueters were crowned. This account of the birth of the rose has it spring spontaneously from the earth in homage to the new-born goddesses, Venus and Minerva, 'the nymph of azure glance'.

Robert Frost, *The Rose Family* (p. 184)
The rose family, otherwise known as the Rosaceae, includes the genera, Malus (apple), Pyrus (pear) and Prunus (plum, cherry, etc.),

as well as Potentilla, Rubus, Sorbus, Cotoneaster, Pyracantha, Alchemilla, Potentilla, Fragaria, Aruncus and Filipendula, among others. (See also poems on pp. 89, 94, 98, and 176.)

Jo Shapcott, *Rosa foetida, Rosa pimpinellifolia, Rosa odorata* (pp. 185–86)
Jo Shapcott was born in 1953 in London. These are three poems selected from her version of 'Les Roses' written in French by Rainer Maria Rilke. *Rosa foetida*, native to Asia minor, is a small bright yellow rose with a perfume so strong as to be offensive. *Rosa pimpinellifolia* is the Scotch or Burnet rose, distinguished by its stems thick-set with prickles and bristles of uneven length, white flowers and black hips. *Rosa odorata* was one of the names given to a type of rose introduced from China by Sir Adrian Hume at the beginning of the nineteenth century, otherwise called 'Hume's Blush Tea-scented China', ancestor of most of our modern hybrid tea roses.

D. H. Lawrence, *Gloire de Dijon* (p. 187)
In 1995 Richard Wilbur wrote in a letter to a friend: 'D. H. Lawrence seems to me to be full of shapeless blather a good deal of the time, but I love the side of him that's concerned with plants and animals and with realising things accurately and feelingly'. Gloire de Dijon is a Noisette climber bred crossing *R. moschata* with *R. chinensis luteus* (?) in 1853; it has Bourbon style blooms of palest flesh-gold, with crimson streaked reverse. (See also poems on pp. 110 and 201.)

Mary Robinson, *Ode to the Snowdrop* (p. 188)
Mary Robinson (1758–1800), called Perdita after her most famous role on the London stage, became the mistress of the Prince of Wales in 1778 and, after sundry other adventures and partial disablement, retired to a cottage in Windsor Great Park, where she

supported her widowed mother and herself by the labours of her pen. This poem originally appeared in her four volume novel, *Walsingham*, published in 1797. The snowdrop, *Galanthus nivalis,* is one of the most celebrated flowers in the British garden hymned by Laetitia Landon, Anna Laetitia Barbauld, Tennyson, Louise Glück, Ted Hughes and George McDonald to name but a few.

Olive Custance, Rainbows – *Forget-me-nots* (p. 190)
Olive Custance (1874–1944) married the reformed Lord Alfred Douglas in 1902, bearing him a son in 1907 and leaving him in 1913. The 'eyes' celebrated were probably Lord Alfred's for the poem was originally published less than a year after her marriage, when the two were still very much in love and often exchanged verses.

Freda Downie, *Aconites* (p. 191)
Downie's are Winter Aconites, *Eranthis hyemalis*, the very first flowers to appear in the New Year. Their green ruffs are the deeply cut bracts that encircle the leafless stems of the flowers that arise from a basal rosette of similarly cut leaves. (See also poems on pp. 52 and 151.)

Seamus Heaney, *Sweetpea* (p. 192)
Heaney celebrates an old woman's sweet peas in the same bitter-sweet mood as Downie her grandmother's garden. The poem begins with the kind of monitory saying typical of Irishwomen of an older generation, moves through the growing process with the children staking the plants and snipping the flowers, to her final illness, and the possible meaning of her sweet pea plot. When Heaney was growing up at Mossbawn, the household relied on the help of his live-in aunt, Mary. (See also poems on pp. 95 and 101.)

Louise Glück, *Hyacinth* (p. 193)

Louise Glück was born in New York City in 1943; she lives in Cambridge, Massachusetts. Hyacinthus is one of the many flower-heroes of mythology struck down in youth to be reborn as flowers. Apollo was teaching Hyacinthus to hurl the discus when the West Wind for jealousy sent it backwards so that it dashed Hyacinthus' brains out. From his blood sprang a dark blue flower, upon which may be read the letters AI AI, either the first letters of his name or Apollo's cry of grief. Graves identifies the flower as the 'Greek hyacinth', which he calls Hyacinthos grapta. No known Hyacinth or muscari species actually corresponds to Homer's description.

Ivor Gurney, *Early Winter* (p. 196)

Gurney identifies both chrysanthemums, Japanese-bred large-flowered hybrids of *Chrysanthemum indicum*, and winter jasmine (*Jasminum nudiflorum*) from Northern China, as the glory of the early winter garden. Japanese species of Acer, Actinidia, Camellia, Chaenomeles, Clematis, Haemerocallis, Hamamelis, Lonicera, Hosta, Lilium, Mahonia and Skimmia are staples for many suburban gardens.

Adrian Henri, *Country Song (Convalaria Majalis)* (p. 197)

Adrian Henri (1938?–2002?) was one of the Liverpool poets, and this poem seems to be set in Lancashire in early summer, when the wild garlic (*Alium oleraceum*), windflowers (*Anemone nemorosa*) and celandines (*Ranunculus ficaria*, the lesser celandine) are in bloom. This poem is mostly self-explanatory; milk-weed is a puzzle, because in England it can be either *Sonchus oleraceus*, the sow-thistle, *Peucedanum palustre*, marsh milk-weed or *Euphorbia helioscopia*, all of which exude milky latex.

Edna St Vincent Millay, *The Strawberry Shrub* (p. 198)
Edna St Vincent Millay (1892–1950) lived most of her life in a
farmhouse at Steepletop, near Austerlitz in upstate New York. Her
strawberry shrub is *Arbutus unedo*.

Anne Ridler, *Columbine and Larkspur* (p. 199)
Ridler's columbines are red and yellow garden hybrids of *Aquilegia*
while the larkspur is the royal blue typical of the species *Consolida*.
(See also poems on pp. 83, 165 and 180.)

D. H. Lawrence, *Red Geranium and Godly Mignonette* (p. 201)
Lawrence argues here that God, having no body, could not
experience the red of the 'geranium', that is to say a zonal
pelargonium, or the smell of the mignonette (*Reseda odorata*).
Heliotropium peruviana was commonly called cherry-pie because it
smelt like a cherry-pie hot from the oven. Mignonette was
championed by the Empress Josephine, hence the wide-spread
adoption of its French name. (See also poems on pp. 110 and 187.)

Kathleen Raine, *The Herm* (p. 203)
A herm is a square pillar surmounted by the bust of Hermes and
sporting male genitals. They were first set up to guard Dionysiac
festivals, and in the early fifth century BC began to appear as
guardians of crossroads in Greece. By Roman times they had
become associated with gardens. (See also poem on p. 164.)

Acknowledgements

The editor and publishers gratefully acknowledge permission to reprint copyright material in this book as follows:

FLEUR ADCOCK: from *Selected Poems 1960-2000*, reprinted by permission of Bloodaxe Books, copyright © 2000. SIMON ARMITAGE: from *Zoom!*, reprinted by permission of Bloodaxe Books, copyright © 1989. JOHN BURNSIDE: from *The Myth of the Twin*, published by Jonathan Cape, reprinted by permission of The Random House Group Ltd, copyright © 1994. DUNCAN BUSH: from *The Hook*, reprinted by permission of Seren Books, copyright © 1997. AMY CLAMPITT: from *Selected Poems*, reprinted by permission of Faber and Faber and Alfred A. Knopf, a division of Random House, Inc, copyright © 1997 The Estate of Amy Clampitt. JOHN CLARE: from *The Cottage Garden*, reprinted by permission of The Curtis Brown Group Ltd, copyright © Eric Robinson. STEWART CONN: from *Stolen Light: Selected Poems*, reprinted by permission of Bloodaxe Books, copyright © 1999. DAVID CONSTANTINE: from *Selected Poems*, reprinted by permission of Bloodaxe Books, copyright © 1991 and *The Pelt of Wasps*, reprinted by permission of Bloodaxe Books, copyright © 1998. E.E. CUMMINGS: from *Complete Poems 1904-1962*, edited by George J. Firmage, reprinted by permission of W. W. Norton & Company, copyright © 1991 by the Trustees for the E.E. Cummings Trust and George James Firmage. WALTER DE LA MARE: from *The Complete Poems*,

Index Of Poets

Index Of First Lines